PENGUIN BOOKS

INTELLIGENT MEMORY

Barry Gordon, M.D., Ph.D., is professor of neurology and cognitive science, founder of the Memory Clinic, and holder of an endowed chair to study the treatment of brain disorders at The John Hopkins Medical Institutions. He is one of the world's leading experts in the study and treatment of memory and language disorders. His first book was *Memory: Remembering and Forgetting in Everyday Life*, about which Oliver Sacks, M.D., remarked: "It is so rich— one can open it almost anywhere, and be captivated at once. [Dr. Gordon has] combined lightness, colloquialism and 'user-friendliness' with depth in a quite remarkable way." Dr. Gordon is the cowriter, coproducer, and host of "Improving Your Memory with Dr. Barry Gordon," a one-hour special public television program.

Lisa Berger is a health and medical writer, and she has written extensively on mental health and mental illness. She is the author of ten books, including *We Heard the Angels of Madness* (with her sister Diane) and *The War on Pain* (with Dr. Scott Fishman).

INTELLIGENT
MEMORY

A Prescription for Improving
Your Memory

Barry Gordon, M.D., Ph.D.
AND
Lisa Berger

PENGUIN BOOKS

PENGUIN BOOKS
Published by the Penguin Group
Penguin Group (USA) Inc., 375 Hudson Street, New York, New York 10014, U.S.A.
Penguin Group (Canada), 10 Alcorn Avenue, Toronto,
    Ontario, Canada M4V 3B2 (a division of Pearson Penguin Canada Inc.)
Penguin Books Ltd, 80 Strand, London WC2R 0RL, England
Penguin Ireland, 25 St Stephen's Green, Dublin 2, Ireland (a division of Penguin Books Ltd)
Penguin Group (Australia), 250 Camberwell Road, Camberwell,
    Victoria 3124, Australia (a division of Pearson Australia Group Pty Ltd)
Penguin Books India Pvt Ltd, 11 Community Centre, Panchsheel Park,
    New Delhi - 110 017, India
Penguin Group (NZ), cnr Airborne and Rosedale Roads, Albany,
    Auckland 1310, New Zealand (a division of Pearson New Zealand Ltd)
Penguin Books (South Africa) (Pty) Ltd, 24 Sturdee Avenue,
    Rosebank, Johannesburg 2196, South Africa

Penguin Books Ltd, Registered Offices: 80 Strand, London WC2R 0RL, England

First published in the United States of America by Viking Penguin,
a member of Penguin Books (USA) Inc. 2003
Published in Penguin Books 2005

10 9 8 7 6 5 4 3 2 1

Copyright © Intelligence Amplification, Inc. and Lisa Berger, 2003
All rights reserved

All illustrations drawn by Dean Gardei unless otherwise credited.

THE LIBRARY OF CONGREE HAS CATALOGUED
THE HARDCOVER EDITION AS FOLLOWS:
Gordon, Barry, M.D.
Intelligent memory : Improve the memory that
makes you smarter / Barry Gordon and Lisa Berger.
p. cm.
ISBN 0-670-03240-9 (hc.)
ISBN 0 14 30.3423 5 (pbk.)
1. Memory.   2. Thought and thinking.   3. Creative thinking.
4. Problem solving.   I. Berger, Lisa.   II. Title.
BF371.G66   2003
153.1'2—dc21   2003050163

Printed in the United States of America

Except in the United States of America, this book is sold subject to the condition
that it shall not, by way of trade or otherwise, be lent, resold, hired out, or otherwise
circulated without the publisher's prior consent in any form of binding or cover
other than that in which it is published and without a similar condition
including this condition being imposed on the subsequent purchaser.

The scanning, uploading and distribution of this book via the Internet or via any other
means without the permission of the publisher is illegal and punishable by law. Please
purchase only authorized electronic editions, and do not participate in or encourage
electronic piracy of copyrighted materials. Your support of the author's rights is appreciated.

To Brett, who never needed instruction,
and to Alex, who always will.

ACKNOWLEDGMENTS

Many people helped us shape the contours of *Intelligent Memory*. Thanks to our expert readers, researchers, and sounding boards Nina Graybill, Susan Gorn, Barbara Jeffrey, Joanne Omang, Edie Stern, Pat Stevens, and Martha Zeiger.

Thanks also to our agent, Gail Ross, for her tireless support and cheerleading, and to our editors, Jane Von Mehren and Jennifer Ehmann, for their patience and gentle nudging.

We are also deeply thankful to the researchers, clinicians, problem-solvers, artists, writers, and others who have helped demonstrate the existence of Intelligent Memory. Only an infinitesimal fraction of the people responsible could be cited or referenced in this book.

Barry owes a perpetual debt to three special families: To the anonymous family who endowed the Therapeutic Cognitive Neuroscience chair that he holds at Johns Hopkins, and who has generously gifted his research. To the late and deeply missed Benjamin E. Miller, and to the gifts and endowment made by Benjamin E. Miller and his family to Johns Hopkins for his research.

And to his own family, including his late father, Bernard Gordon, and his mother, Blanche, for instilling life-long motivation, fostering intellectual fearlessness, and tempering the mix with practical wisdom and loving criticism.

Barry thanks his wife, Renée, for gracefully permitting the effort required, despite her perfect memory (far better than his) of what the *last* book entailed.

Lisa thanks her family for everything: her sisters, Cathy and Diane, for being there when she needed them most, Dad and Ginny for their worrying and fussing, Peter for swimming tips, and Donny for comic relief.

CONTENTS

INTRODUCTION

The memory you think you want is not the memory you need the most.

Almost everyone complains about being unable to recall people's names, find misplaced purses or car keys, or remember why they started driving to the store. These problems revolve around a type of memory called ordinary memory.

However, there is another kind of memory, Intelligent Memory, that is just as important. It is what fails people when they feel that they don't think as quickly or as cleverly as they'd like to. They feel left behind when friends and relatives solve problems better than they do or get the joke or see the point faster. They wonder, "Why didn't I think of that? Why didn't I anticipate that problem? Why didn't I see the answer? Why couldn't I connect the dots?"

Intelligent Memory is the memory that "glues" our thinking—and the pieces of our ordinary memory—together. Intelligent Memory is both a thought or idea as well as a cognitive process, yielding what is often called critical or creative thinking. It's composed of three elements: pieces of memory (namely: experiences, information, and knowledge); the connections between these pieces; and the distinctive mental processing that mixes and matches the pieces and connections, creating more sophisticated thinking. Unlike ordinary memory, which weakens with age, Intelligent Memory can be strengthened with advancing years and improved by experience.

Although Intelligent Memory plays a role in every facet of our mental life, it has been largely overlooked as an area for improvement. Most people focus on developing their ordinary memory without considering the possibility that their mental lapses might stem from another source. This neglect is largely because Intelligent Memory does not conform to most people's idea of what memory is and how it works. Unlike the workings of ordinary memory, Intelligent Memory's operations are hidden and usually very rapid.

Most people assume that ordinary memory is responsible for one's level of intelligence, so if they have problems thinking, they blame ordinary memory and look no further. Actually, there's little direct connection between remembering facts and being intelligent. Those who can remember lots of facts are not always the brightest. Some individuals, such as some of those with autism, can have an astonishing memory for facts but little useful intelligence. People who win memory competitions are not necessarily able to outsmart those who don't win. And people who have almost no ordinary memory, such as those with true amnesia, still retain their intelligence.

Intelligent Memory fuels your intelligence. It is a ubiquitous and automatic part of your mental processing, and the machinery that drives "smart" thinking. Intelligent Memory can make you smart in many ways. It can improve a vast range of everyday activities, from negotiating with a boss to making a hobby more fun. In a study of how people learn to pick winning racehorses, one of the most successful handicappers had an eighth-grade education and an IQ of 92. While he probably struggled with school, he was at the head of the class at the racetrack.

As a neuroscientist, most of my professional life has been spent trying to understand how our minds work, what can go wrong, and how they can be fixed or improved. Much of my work has focused on memory, in part because memory is so important to the workings of our minds. My earlier book, *Memory: Remembering and Forgetting in Everyday Life*, explained people's ordinary memory and how they could improve it. I only briefly referred to Intelligent Memory there, and not even by name. This was because most of my patients believed that ordinary memory was the source of their problems and wanted to know more about it. But around this time, the roles of ordinary memory versus Intelligent Memory hit home for me with an urgency I never could have imagined.

My son, Alex, was born shortly before I starting working on *Memory*. He should have grown into a normal little boy by the time it was published, but he didn't. He never learned to speak, and even had to be helped to eat. His formal diagnosis was autism with severe developmental delay. Today, even some of the simplest tasks of everyday life—retrieving a dropped object by going under a table and not over it, for example—are immensely challenging to Alex. His IQ is so low it is almost unmeasurable. Yet he can operate a videotape machine like a pro. Confronted with Alex's problems and with his curious pattern of weaknesses and strengths, I had to ask myself why some things were so hard for him, yet so easy for us. How does our brain solve these little puzzles? Why couldn't he? And why could he do some other things so much better than I could?

The answer applies not just to Alex but to everyone: Intelligent Memory is what makes most of what we learn in life stick. It helps us write a strategic report for work, decide which investment to make for retirement, prepare a spur-of-the-moment dinner for guests, persuade a teenage daughter to stop smoking, plan a surprise birthday party for a spouse, negotiate a home-remodeling contract, and talk a store manager into accepting an exchange. It helps us solve problems, gives us insight, and allows us to think creatively.

Why should you stop worrying about ordinary memory and focus on Intelligent Memory? Increasingly, the world is demanding that we think better. There's an intellectual race going on, especially in the workplace. Highly competitive companies are including critical or creative thinking tests as part of their interviews for new employees. While portions of these tests relate to traditional ideas of intelligence, sizeable parts of them probe a person's ability to think quickly and creatively. One company head asks job applicants to teach him something he doesn't know, "to see if they're good at explaining and if they know anything." Many such tests ask potential employees to tap into Intelligent Memory.

Even if job applications don't require Intelligent Memory, our lives do. It enables us to surmount and surpass everyday problems and can enhance the quality of our knowledge, so that we can better understand and appreciate literature, movies, cartoons, even advertisements. Intelligent Memory can also generate creative ideas. These ideas may be as simple as witty wordplay or as sophisticated as an original way to explain a complicated procedure. Intelligent Memory deepens insight into people and situations. An active Intelligent Memory draws from a wide repository of stored images and ideas, and these add breadth and depth to our insights. Things make more sense, whether it's the nuances of an annual report or understanding why a boyfriend dumped us.

While the process of changing the way people think about problems and solve everyday dilemmas is neither simple nor easy, the results can be striking. We are surrounded by everyday conveniences inspired by Intelligent Memory. Who hasn't used a suitcase with wheels, a Walkman, overnight delivery, or frequent-flyer miles and wondered, "Why didn't I think of that?" The answer is that most people can.

Smart thinking is not an inexplicable spark of mental energy over which we have no control. It isn't only for geniuses. Quite the opposite: Intelligent Memory encompasses mental tools that can be acquired and sharpened. It is not fixed at birth and is not unchangeable. It grows over a lifetime. Its content and capacity are limitless and it can take any form or direction. While biology establishes where your Intelligent Memory starts, you determine where it goes. With instruction and practice, almost anyone can learn to think better.

While age-related ordinary memory impairment begins to creep up on us in our fifties, causing us to forget facts and faces, Intelligent Memory gets better with the years. As we add experience and knowledge to our minds, we are accumulating more Intelligent Memory. This accumulation continues as long as we let it: into our fifties, sixties, seventies, and beyond.

The more you use your Intelligent Memory in your daily living, the more often you will find ways to apply it and the more versatile it becomes. It gets stronger as you call on your memories and the connections between them. As you pump up your Intelligent Memory, the thinking it produces becomes more accessible. Smart ideas pop to mind more quickly.

Intelligent Memory, for many people, is at the heart of success in life. It's not the only factor—personality and luck play big roles—but it's perhaps the most important one that we can influence.

This book is unlike any other memory book you may have read. It won't help you play Trivial Pursuit or remember everyone's name at a party, but it will help you better solve your everyday problems and learn to think better and more creatively. It will synthesize the evidence and eliminate the jargon to show you how good thinking works, and how Intelligent Memory can improve it.

INTELLIGENT
MEMORY

CHAPTER 1

What Is Intelligent Memory?

Take a moment to contemplate how you think. Every thought is made up of many steps. Our mind is making rapid-fire connections between bits of memory, each taking a fraction of a second to produce. We use two very different kinds of memory in our thinking. The first is the kind of memory people are most familiar with, ordinary memory. Ordinary memory is responsible for remembering specific times, dates, places, people, events, and facts. It is what most people are referring to when they think or talk about their "memory." Because ordinary memory is a conscious process, we are constantly aware of it, when it works and, especially, when it doesn't. It is our ordinary memory that fails us when we forget where we put our car keys.

The second category, however, is a much greater kind of memory called Intelligent Memory. Intelligent Memory is the memory that contains everything else we know about our car keys, like what they're for, what they resemble, and what they can be used for besides starting a car. It is Intelligent Memory, not ordinary memory, that you're using to read these words. Your Intelligent Memory is sprinting along, translating the marks on the page into words you can recognize, and figuring out what the words mean.

While ordinary memory is where we keep specific facts, Intelligent Memory is where we keep connections and meanings. Ordinary memory is conscious and relatively slow—we are often aware of the effort involved in trying to remember a name or a date—but Intelligent Memory is quick, effortless, and usually unconscious. It's responsible for almost everything we do with our senses, our minds, and our muscles. But in particular, it's the engine powering most of our intelligence. That is why we call it Intelligent Memory.

Each of us, no matter how poor our ordinary memory, has an extraordinary amount of Intelligent Memory, and we use it all the time. We don't have to strain or force Intelligent Memory into action, as we do with ordinary memory. It creates ideas that pop to mind effortlessly. It sparks answers and solutions without us having to ponder them.

A perfect example of all the mental activity that goes into Intelligent Memory comes from Sherlock Holmes. Here is Dr. Watson's account of the first time he met Holmes:

> "Dr. Watson, Mr. Sherlock Holmes," said Stamford, introducing us.
>
> "How are you?" he said cordially, gripping my hand with a strength for which I should hardly have given him credit. "You have been in Afghanistan, I perceive."
>
> "How on earth did you know that?" I asked in astonishment.
>
> Holmes replied: ". . . From long habit the train of thoughts ran so swiftly through my mind that I arrived at the conclusion without being conscious of intermediate steps. There were such steps, however. The train of reasoning ran, 'Here is a gentleman of a medical type, but with the air of a military man. Clearly an army doctor, then. He has just come from the tropics, for his face is dark, and that is not the natural tint of his skin, for his wrists are fair. He has undergone hardship and sickness, as his haggard face says clearly. His left arm has been injured. He holds it in a stiff and unnatural manner. Where in the tropics could an English army doctor have seen much hardship and got his arm wounded? Clearly in Afghanistan.' The whole train of thought did not occupy a second."

Holmes's Intelligent Memory sharpened his perceptions, made connections, considered several inferences from those connections, and found an explanation that fit them all in a fraction of a second. While this example is fictional, it demonstrates how a good Intelligent Memory functions—observing and thinking simultaneously, moving so rapidly between memories and thoughts that it barely leaves a detectable trace of its operations.

PICKING UP WHERE ORDINARY MEMORY LEAVES OFF

Sherlock Holmes's ordinary memory could not have accomplished such a feat. It contains only specific facts, new faces, and dates and times, and it works slowly, often requiring a great deal of mental energy to produce a fact or an idea. It is the lightning-quick connectivity of Intelligent Memory that is necessary to produce Holmes's brilliant deductions.

Here are some examples that show where ordinary memory leaves off, or fails us, and Intelligent Memory steps in to generate an idea that saves the day. As you read on, you'll learn how it actually accomplishes this mental legerdemain.

- You forget where you put your car keys and search everywhere for them. You then suddenly remember that you put a spare key in a magnetic box under the car years ago.
- You can't recall the name of someone who greets you on the street, but his conversation implies that he knows your spouse, and that suddenly gives you his name.
- Arriving at the grocery store, you realize that you've forgotten your shopping list. However, as you walk through the store and glance at the shelves, you remember what you need.
- You drop your glasses behind a sofa too heavy to move. You can't figure out how to retrieve them at first, but then you have an idea: You undo a wire coat hanger and use it to snag them.
- You're waiting for a friend in front of a department store. Your friend told you he had business to do on the fifth floor. While

waiting, you idly look around. You notice that the building has four stories, and immediately realize that you must be in the wrong place because your friend was going to be on the fifth floor.

- You're in a field trying to help your son with his model rocket, but you're as much of a novice as he is. Both of you are desperate to find help. Another father and son are doing rocketry on the same field. You overhear that father tell his son that the cloud cover looks like it's at about 5,000 feet. You realize that this man knows rockets and can help you and your son, even though your son doesn't see the connection.

- This cartoon makes you smile before you know why:

(ZIGGY © 1988 ZIGGY AND FRIENDS, INC. Reprinted with permission of UNIVERSAL PRESS SYNDICATE. All rights reserved.)

HOW IT WORKS

Intelligent Memory is at work almost everywhere. It directs our senses to help us see, hear, move, smell, and taste. It powers much of our higher thinking, including problem solving, social skills, and creativity. It is normally almost invisible, but you can learn to recognize its workings. To give you a sense of how it functions, we'll start with how it sees and interprets a relatively simple concept, such as a visual image. What do you see in the following picture?

Do you see the Dalmatian looking toward the left-hand margin? You may see it instantly or only after a second or two. If you did see the Dalmatian, the visual parts of your Intelligent Memory enabled you to do so. Since there are only splotches of black and white in the picture, your visual Intelligent Memory matched the splotches with all the shapes and forms you have ever seen. In a split second, it sorted through the millions of images in your memory and found that the best fit was a Dalmatian.

You won't see a Dalmatian in the picture if you've never seen this type of dog before. However, if you have seen a Dalmatian, even if you don't remember seeing it, then you have an Intelligent Memory of it. That's because Intelligent Memory "learns" automatically every time it is used, whether it captures a visual image, like the Dalmatian, or generates complicated ideas. It arises from the activity of nerve cells and their connections in your brain, which learn more every time they are activated. Everything they experience changes them a little and becomes part of the mosaic of nerve connections that produces Intelligent Memory.

This activation of nerve cells, and the consequent learning, can occur even if it is unintentional. Though you never set out to memorize all the dogs you've ever seen, your brain automatically embeds them in its visual Intelligent Memory. So while you may have forgotten that Pongo and Perdita were the Dalmatians in *101 Dalmatians,* the essence of their Dalmatian looks were locked into the visual part of your Intelligent Memory. Once that Dalmatian is in there, the process of gathering together the blotches on the page, comparing them against everything in memory, and finding that a Dalmatian is the best match takes less than half a second in most people.

The Dalmatian example highlights the basic hallmarks of Intelligent Memory:

- It really is a function of memory; you have to have had the experience in your mind to tap into it or build on it.
- It works very quickly. Its basic steps take only fractions of a second.
- Many parts of Intelligent Memory can work at once. Even during sleep, some parts of your Intelligent Memory are churning.
- Intelligent Memory is always learning. Whenever it works, it remembers what it is doing, automatically.
- Most of the time, you are not aware of it working. You're aware of the image or idea that it generates, but not of the process it goes through to produce that image or idea.
- You can consciously steer some parts of your Intelligent Memory and make them learn what and how you want them to learn.

Try this next picture. What do you see?

Despite the fact that the zebra is harder to see than the Dalmatian for most people, if you saw it, you probably saw it faster this time because of your earlier experience with the Dalmatian picture. Chances are you probably didn't have much experience looking at blobs before, but searching the blobs in the Dalmatian picture taught you how to look at them more effectively and stimulated more visual images in your Intelligent Memory. As a result, the mental operations you used to look at the picture and to match it against the images in your mind also became more efficient. Your Intelligent Memory just improved. And it did so without any deliberate mental effort on your part.

THREE PARTS OF THE ENGINE

Intelligent Memory has three major components: pieces of information, connections between the pieces, and the mental processes that manage the pieces and connections. (The processes are themselves made of the same basic stuff, pieces and connections.) It's like a network of computers, managed by a network administrator, and the network administrator is a computer too. There is memory in every part of this system, so every part can learn from experience or can be taught.

We possess a vast number of pieces of information in our Intelligent Memory. Your mental pictures of Dalmatians and zebras, as well as of any dogs or wild animals that you've ever seen, are pieces of information. Some pieces are facts ("Washington, D.C., is the capital of the United States"). However, most pieces are not facts; they're sensory perceptions and visual images, like the feel of velvet or what your high school English teacher looked like. Or they're concepts and knowledge, like honesty. Skills are also pieces of information. They can be as simple as how to turn the key in a lock or as complex as how to ride a bike, shoot pool, or play golf.

The connections between pieces of information are dense webs that link to form complex ideas. We possess a connection between the sound of the word "brain" and the letters B-R-A-I-N. We have connections linking what our senses detect, like a cold nose, a panting tongue, or a wagging tail, and concepts, like the mental picture of an eager dog. A television, a VCR, and a remote control are similarly connected to produce the notion of a couch potato. These connections were all learned. There was a first exposure to them, when they were new to us, but once they were learned, they became part of Intelligent Memory.

At any one time, most of the pieces of information in our heads, and the connections between them, lie dormant. Similar to a computer that has not been turned on, a part of our memory has not been awakened. This was probably the case with all your pieces of information about dogs before you saw the picture of the Dalmatian. But if something triggers latent pieces and connections—like seeing a picture related to them—they become activated. Once activated, they trigger other pieces through the connections in Intelligent Memory. This activation can be automatic and run on its own. If you saw a Dalmatian when you looked at the blobs on the paper, a flood of activation went in the right direction and wound up triggering the image of a Dalmatian in your mind.

The third part of your Intelligent Memory, the memory processing administrator, didn't have to do anything with these activations. But if it took you a few seconds to see the Dalmatian, the memory processing administrator went to work. It recognized that nothing was connecting and began directing the activation of pieces and the flow of information. Because it was working so hard, you were probably aware of the feeling of "searching" through your memory. That feeling was the memory processing administrator determining what parts of your memory had been searched and checking to see if anything came from that search. If the search did yield information, the administrator made an extra effort to lock it into your memory.

Another way of thinking about what goes on in Intelligent Memory is that it is like connecting dots to form a picture. The dots are pieces or ideas, the lines between them are your connections or associations. The lines can coalesce into larger fragments, and these fragments can merge to form a whole thought. This whole thought may be a visual image, a piece of knowledge, an idea, or even the solution to a problem.

Individual pieces, their connections, and the mental processing that orchestrates them generally work together so they appear to be a single cognitive event. That's what happens when ideas or concepts "pop" to mind. Your ability to read these words is an example. When you were a small child and unable yet to read, written English could have been Cyrillic for all you knew. You had to learn about the lines that form each letter and recognize each group of lines as a familiar pattern. Now, not only are many lines molded into single pieces, which you think of as individual letters, but collections of letters have also become pieces—words—in Intelligent Memory. And if you're an experienced reader, collections of words have become pieces loaded with meaning: "Fourscore and seven years ago," "It was a dark and stormy night," "The dog ate my homework," "The check is in the mail."

Each combination of pieces and connections, and the processing that meshes them, functions like a miniature mind within our brain. These "miniminds" are capable of thinking for themselves swiftly and usually below the surface of our consciousness. Many miniminds can be active in the brain at once, monitoring and making decisions. The miniminds that deal with reading, for instance, quickly give us the meanings of words, sentences, and passages. Sherlock Holmes's miniminds processed large pieces of information to produce a deduction about the meaning of Watson's features. Miniminds boost the power of our conscious mind, which is pretty much limited to one thought at a time.

This mental processing packages complex perceptions, ideas, and skills into your Intelligent Memory. Remember, it remembers! Each new arrangement or packaging of pieces and connections makes our Intelligent Memory larger and stronger: larger because a new concept has been added to your mental arsenal, and stronger because once-separate pieces are now a single, distinctive idea that is readily available.

BECOMING A BETTER THINKER

Intelligent Memory thinks on its own, automatically. But you can guide it so that it will work even better. Cramming your brain with lots of facts may help your ordinary memory, but it may make only a modest improvement in your Intelligent Memory. The best way to improve your Intelligent Memory is to strengthen the mental processes that manage it. These processes are paying attention, storing memories or pieces, building connections, finding the right memories or pieces, and tuning the entire system by testing your results as you go along.

Since Intelligent Memory learns automatically, improving it doesn't have to be work—it can be fun. When people think slowly or produce mediocre ideas, it's often because they haven't tuned up their intelligent memories properly. They've neglected the mental activities that give Intelligent Memory a workout and make it perform better. Good thinkers don't neglect these mental workouts. The situation is similar to the difference between amateurs and professionals in sports. The amateur swimmer rarely thinks of the specific parts of the motion that moves her from one side of the pool to the other. The professional swimmer, however, mentally breaks down the main components of a stroke—like the elbow lift, catch, pull, and hip rotation—and considers how she uses them while she's swimming. That way, she makes each movement better, and makes them all work together better.

When we look back at the several examples presented earlier in this chapter, we can now see that a well-honed Intelligent Memory unconsciously sought out the connection between, for example, the lost key and the spare key hidden long before. Intelligent Memory took the threads from the conversation in the street, and found the link between spouse and stranger. At the grocery store, Intelligent Memory was triggered by the items on the shelves.

As Holmes points out, it was practice that made his Intelligent Memory work so quickly, smoothly, and correctly. The first steps toward improving your Intelligent Memory are understanding more about how it works and identifying where it is not working as well as it might. In the next chapter, we'll give you a chance to feel your own Intelligent Memory and test how well it's working.

CHAPTER 2

Testing Your Intelligent Memory

When Intelligent Memory is working best, it's faster than conscious appreciation. Its connections skip from thought to thought. The light that flashes in your head—the "Aha!" moment—comes from completing a chain of connections. Since Intelligent Memory races so quickly and quietly and learns so fast, it's hard to observe it in action. It's also particularly hard to test it in yourself. So that you can, we're going to use a few tricks.

One trick is to give you questions or problems we hope you've never seen before. This way, we can make your Intelligent Memory sputter and balk. As it thrashes around, it may slow down and strain enough so you can get a glimpse of how it's working. The other trick is to use the speed of IM against itself. We're going to give you problems that will bring your IM to a dead stop, make it veer suddenly, or even make two chains of thought collide.

This test doesn't have to be stressful. In fact, it should be fun. It uses the same process that comedians, cartoonists, and good writers do to create humor. Robin Williams excels at taking our thoughts and twisting them, making them hit each other. Banging ideas and impressions together can be very entertaining, so we expect some of these questions will be too. And the collision of thoughts in Intelligent Memory can also spark creative ideas. Think Salvador Dalí or Andy Warhol. So don't be surprised if the test actually inspires you a bit.

Some questions here may seem unsolvable while others may be a snap. That's because a problem that one person's Intelligent Memory flits through automatically and rapidly may briefly perplex another person and completely baffle a third person. Remember the Dalmatian? Some people never see it. They may experience what the Spanish call a *rompecabeza*—literally, a "headbreaker." Don't despair—every one has their *rompecabezas*. Nevertheless, there's a good chance the answers to many of these questions will be obvious to you.

The questions are probes that show you where you do, or don't, have Intelligent Memory. We describe what each reveals about your Intelligent Memory and its operations. Since even the simplest vignette or joke calls on dozens if not hundreds of Intelligent Memory operations, we describe only the salient pieces of what happens, or should happen, in your mind as you confront each question.

The items we've chosen are designed to reveal the universal mental processes that are central to an effective Intelligent Memory: paying attention, expanding scratch-pad (temporary) memory, storing memories, sparking connections, finding memories, and tuning thinking. As you'll discover, however, no question can isolate a single one of these processes. It's impossible to engage your visual attention, for instance, without also causing your brain to make connections between pieces you've stored. Nevertheless, the questions will give you a usable yardstick for measuring strengths and weaknesses. Keep in mind also that there are vast domains of Intelligent Memory that cannot be tested in a book. You may be an intuitive tennis player, a born musician, a wonderful painter, or a talented carpenter. These abilities will probably not come into play in here. But, the same general principles are at work.

To give you a way to assess whether you are using your Intelligent Memory and to what extent, we've set up a simple scoring system for each question:

A. Circle letter A if you get the answer instantly and without thinking. A quick response is a sure sign of Intelligent Memory. The connection or clash of thoughts happened immediately.

B. Circle letter B if it takes you a few seconds before you get the answer. This response shows that your Intelligent Memory isn't

coming up with an answer fast enough, so your ordinary thinking has to take over while your Intelligent Memory percolates.

C. What answer? What are you talking about? Nothing clicks,
either automatically or consciously. If this happens, circle letter C. The Intelligent Memory needed for this particular question may be outside your experience, interest, or thinking style.

Ready?

ATTENTION

1. What catches your eye in this drawing?

A.	B.	C.
Got it instantly.	Took a few seconds.	What?

You don't know what you're looking for in this picture, but your Intelligent Memory will guide your eyes for you. (Did you see the one sad
face?)

Paying attention is critical for all memory. Paying attention and
learning build on themselves. The more you pay attention, the more you
learn, and the more you recognize as familiar, the better your Intelligent
Memory can sort out what's unfamiliar. It can be hard work but your

Intelligent Memory can make it easier because it notices things while your deliberate thoughts are elsewhere. Intelligent Memory does this by applying an automatic, unconscious form of attention. If you've previously saved information in your Intelligent Memory, such as smiley faces, then it can check for them automatically. The one face that's sad will pop out without your having to plod through all of them.

2. Watson and Sherlock Holmes go camping. They pitch their tent under the stars and go to sleep. In the middle of the night, Holmes wakes Watson up and says, "Look up at the stars, and tell me what you deduce."

Watson ponders the view for a minute. "I see millions of stars," he replies. "Even if only a few of them have planets, and even if only a few of those planets are like Earth, there must be life out there. That's what I deduce."

Holmes looks at him aghast, and exclaims . . .

A. Got it instantly.	B. Took a few seconds.	C. What?

What Holmes blurts out is, "Watson, you idiot! Someone stole our tent!" Watson wasn't really wrong, he just missed the obvious. His conjecture was plausible but the result of a different set of connections than Holmes had made. He didn't make the connections Holmes did between seeing the stars, the absence of their tent, and the fact that if the tent was missing, someone must have taken it.

Any piece of information—such as the ability to see the stars—has many possible relevant connections. Intelligent attention comes from identifying which connection is *most* relevant at any one time and depends on prior experience, degree of attention, and expectations. Holmes's deduction that the tent had been stolen was the most relevant and practical observation. Watson's less relevant observation stemmed from his eagerness to show off and perhaps also was a result of his medical background, which helped to blind him to the obvious crime that Holmes saw immediately. The lesson here for us is to pause before we extrapolate from what our attention made obvious.

3. Examine this sketch. Do you see the faces?

A.	B.	C.
Got it instantly.	Took a few seconds.	What?

Detecting the man and the woman hidden in this drawing taps into your ability to keep options open in your mind so that you can attend to any possibility. To see them, you have not only to pay attention to the right details, but also let your mind's eye work at several different scales. The man's face pokes out from behind the window, facing right. (It's easier to see if you tip the picture to the right.) The woman's face is much smaller, and is poking out from beneath the ferns.

4. Should a man be allowed to marry his widow's sister?

A.	B.	C.
Got it instantly.	Took a few seconds.	What?

This is a test of how deeply you pay attention to words and meanings. To get the right answer, you have to be a careful reader. Quickly scanning the words usually produces a wrong answer, namely the assumption that of course a man should be able to marry his dead wife's sister. A more thoughtful reading reveals that it refers to *his own* "widow's" sister, meaning that the man himself is dead. So the question makes no sense.

Most of the time, we don't have to pay much attention to individual words and their exact meanings. In most everyday conversation, their meanings are automatically understood by our brain. And there's often a great deal of context and redundancy to help us figure out what is meant even if we don't hear a certain word or understand it properly. But when taking a test such as this one, you need to pay closer attention to wording. You have to focus more and rev up your reading concentration to make sure that everything makes sense.

SCRATCH-PAD MEMORY

1. Read about Oceana and answer the question. Later you'll be asked another question about it.

> Oceana is a small, snowy country noted for vast elk herds and rocky coastline. Its primary exports are leather goods, especially exquisitely made furry boots, and gourmet limpets. Its people spend whole lifetimes harvesting the limpets, which requires constant stooping. As a result, their backs have become so curved that the average Oceanian is less than five feet tall.

- Which of the following statements is most likely to be true?

  Oceanians love to go on picnics.
  Oceanians have lots of back problems.
  Oceanians are skilled horsemen.
  Oceanians wear furry boots.

A.	B.	C.
Got it instantly.	Took a few seconds.	What?

This question tests your scratch-pad memory, also known as working or short-term memory. This is the temporary memory we use to get through the basics of the day; it remembers individual, vital pieces of information, such as where you set down your coffee cup or the phone number you just heard. Scratch-pad memory is relatively small, holding around seven chunks of information at any one time, and is constantly updating itself by either dropping items to make room for more or shifting an item to long-term memory. Although scratch-pad memory also plays a role in ordinary memory, Intelligent Memory does more with it—it uses the information held in scratch-pad memory to draw conclusions or inferences.

To get the best answer here, you needed to remember a number of facts from the paragraph and then extrapolate to what may be the most accurate conclusion, "Oceanians wear furry boots." The statement about back problems was included as deliberate interference—that is, words that would tickle your memory and produce an answer but not the best one.

What's most important about your answer is how quickly you produced it and where it came from. If you were able to get the answer rapidly, you pulled information from your scratch-pad memory and derived your answer from that information with your Intelligent Memory. Good! That's the most efficient way. If it took you longer or if you had to go back and search the statements again, your scratch-pad memory was not up to the task. That's not necessarily a problem, but it does suggest you have to consider ways of expanding your scratch-pad because it's important for many things you want to do with your mind. If you knew all the facts but still had problems with the answer, then you need to improve how your Intelligent Memory makes inferences and judges results.

2. How are three of these objects related?

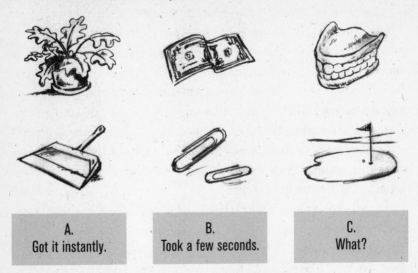

A.	B.	C.
Got it instantly.	Took a few seconds.	What?

This question tests how well your Intelligent Memory ferrets out connections. There is no single right answer. Three of these objects are green. Did you find that connection? Perhaps you strung items together by imagining a rich golfer who's losing his teeth. Or, perhaps you thought of sweeping sand and paper clips off the floor into the dustpan, after moving the potted plant and then collecting your paycheck. (OK, that's five items.) The important questions to ask yourself are how fast were you at making connections and how creative were those connections? The answers will tell you a great deal about how the parts of your own Intelligent Memory work.

To find possible connections among any three items, your Intelligent Memory had to activate every feature of each item and hold them in scratch-pad memory while it sorted through common qualities. At the same time, it had to discard qualities that fit only two items since you were searching for three. It sounds like a major job and it is, but for many people, it takes less than a second. This is because the processing is not only fast but different threads of it operate simultaneously.

It would have been fastest if all six images had already been in your scratch-pad memory at once. Such a situation might be easy for someone trained as a visual artist because this is a part of Intelligent Memory that's been strengthened. Those of us who haven't had the training may have struggled with a smaller scratch-pad memory for visual items.

You had to make connections from aspects of the pictures. How many did you come up with? How straightforward were they? How bizarre? Bizarre connections might be really creative or just bizarre. Here, it didn't matter, just as long as you found commonality between three items. But if this were a piece of art you had created, you would want your audience to be able to appreciate the connections.

Your connections may have happened automatically or deliberately, or both. If automatic, the answer popped into your head. If deliberate, you examined your thoughts, checked if they answered the question, and sent them in a different direction if you needed to make another try. This was your memory processing administrator at work, relatively slowly and deliberately, because the automatic connections hadn't worked. Over time and with repetition, the memory processing administrator may be able to make some connections automatic and work on autopilot next time.

3. This question is similar to the previous one. Can you find three objects that have a feature in common?

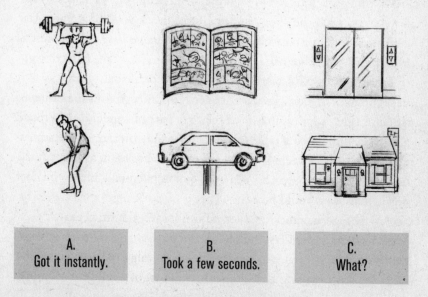

A.	B.	C.
Got it instantly.	Took a few seconds.	What?

One answer is that the elevator, car, and house all have doors and hold people. Or maybe you saw that the weight lifter, elevator, and car lift all raise things. Or you may have found other connections. Any are correct.

This question asks you to hold things in memory, activate their connections, and identify the ones that three of them have in common. This identification can be automatic or you may need to use your memory processing administrator. What differentiates this question from the previous one is that you've been primed. Every part of your Intelligent Memory learned a bit from the previous example, so every part should be working a bit better. It is now easier for you to find the common thread. This is an example of how your Intelligent Memory can learn to work better.

4. How long does it take you to read and understand this?

A STARFISH CAN BE CUT INTO MANY PIECES AND EACH PIECE WILL GROW INTO A WHOLE STARFISH.

A. Got it instantly.	B. Took a few seconds.	C. What?

It says: "A starfish can be cut into many pieces and each piece will grow into a whole starfish."

Normally, a skilled reader will not find a particular typeface a barrier. The mind makes quick adjustments in order to read the different typeface. The learning that takes place is part of Intelligent Memory. The more unfamiliar a typeface, the slower the learning, or the adjustment step, in our memory. And when the translation is slowed, the meanings of the words are fed into our scratch-pad memory more slowly than they would be otherwise.

Scratch-pad memory holds the meaning of each word that is deciphered so you can understand the sentence as a whole. When reading is slowed, scratch-pad memory may fade by the time you get to the end of a sentence. Reading and also understanding the sentence becomes harder. Is that what you experienced? How quickly your reading speed picked up indicates how well your Intelligent Memory performed. How readily you understood the sentence, even if you still were having problems reading, is an indication of how well your scratch-pad memory is working.

This is also an example of how one part of Intelligent Memory can compensate for another. The better your understanding of words and the better your scratch-pad memory, the less you have to depend upon reading each individual word. This is how a person with dyslexia can compensate for difficulty reading words. Conversely, the better you are at reading words by themselves, the less of a strain you put on your scratch-pad memory or your ability to guess the meanings of the words together. Skilled readers are usually good at each step of this process: decoding words, scratch-pad memory, and guessing the meaning of what is being discussed.

Want to see if your Intelligent Memory just learned? Read this:

THE UMBRELLA ORIGINATED IN ANCIENT EGYPT WHERE MEMBERS OF THE ROYAL FAMILY AND NOBLES USED IT AS A SYMBOL OF RANK. ITS USE AS PROTECTION FROM RAIN CAME MANY YEARS LATER.

This sentence is set in the same typeface, but now it's somewhat familiar. It says, "The umbrella originated in ancient Egypt where members of the royal family and nobles used it as a symbol of rank. Its use as protection from rain came many years later." You should have read the typeface somewhat faster this time and with less effort because your Intelligent Memory has learned how to read it. As a result, you understand its parts better and go to the meaning of the sentence more directly.

MEMORY STORAGE

1. Without looking back to the previous question about Oceana, can you tell which of these statements about Oceana is most likely to be true?

It's cold in Oceana.
Oceanians have long lifetimes.
Elk outnumber the people in Oceana.
Oceanians love to cook.

| A. Got it instantly. | B. Took a few seconds. | C. What? |

The most plausible answer is "It's cold in Oceana," although it is also reasonable to infer that "Elk outnumber the people in Oceana." Getting a correct as well as a speedy answer are important tests of your Intelligent Memory. Since the paragraph about Oceana never directly stated either of the possible answers, you had to make deductions from the facts that Oceana was snowy and had vast herds of elk. At the same time, you had to discard the incorrect choices. Lifetimes were mentioned, but not in terms of how long Oceanians lived. And the statement never said anything about cooking. So, to answer this question, you had to not only remember what was said about Oceana, but also extrapolate from what you were not told.

If the answer choices had been based on what had been directly stated, and you had been warned earlier that you were going to be tested, this item would have been more of a test of ordinary memory. Since you weren't warned, this was a test of how well your Intelligent Memory learned from the previous question.

This was also a test of how well you make connections. You might have made the connection with cold when you read about how Oceana was snowy. The association would have been a natural one, and your Intelligent Memory would have stored it as part of the web of associations about Oceana. If this had happened, you would have quickly answered this question because the answer was already in your head. If the connections you needed were not already in your mind, you would have used possible answers as starting points for a search of your Intelligent Memory. This search could have been automatic: Just seeing the word "cold" might have triggered a memory of a snowy Oceana. The other possible answers would have triggered little or nothing at all. If that were the case, your answer would also have come quickly.

It's also possible that none of the possible answers prompted a thought about Oceana. In this case, your memory process administrator would have guided your search. Instead of trying to remember the meaning of what you read, it might have directed your memory to the words you saw, making the search fairly slow. You still might have gotten the right answer, but it would have been a more laborious process than if your Intelligent Memory had been more engaged.

2. Do you understand this?

"Hough dou peapel rede gnew wirds?"

A.	B.	C.
Got it instantly.	Took a few seconds.	What?

This question forced you to reprogram the steps your Intelligent Memory takes in the reading process. While the letters and letter combinations were familiar, the "words" were not. You couldn't find their meanings in your mental dictionary, so you had to sound them out. This is not easy. For each word, your Intelligent Memory had to come up with the sounds each letter or letter combination might represent, then find what real words corresponded to the collection of sounds. It had to ignore false trails (the "g" that begins the "gnew" isn't pronounced, and "hough" could be pronounced several different ways), and after your Intelligent Memory came up with the sound of each "word," you then had to listen to the sounds to hear what they meant.

This perception-translation process is where Intelligent Memory excels. It also excels at having many of these processes working in parallel, simultaneously, almost without your awareness.

To understand this sentence ("How do people read new words?"), you had to change the way you read and remember. Skilled readers normally read for meaning and may not "hear" the sounds of the words in their mind. This is the faster method of reading. When you were a child just starting to read, you understood spoken words but had to decipher the squiggles on the page. You were probably first taught to decipher them by the sounds of their letters ("B" is pronounced "bee"). You heard yourself speaking and you figured the meaning from there. You probably also discovered that English is not very lawful in relating spelling to sounds (try sounding out "yacht"). Also, speaking to yourself as you read is slow. And there are many words we read that we're unlikely to hear spoken often. So, over a period of years, you learned to read written symbols directly for their meaning. Thus, whether it's English or Chinese, the Intelligent Memory of a skilled reader has learned all of the associations and tricks, and performs them quickly, effortlessly, and usually unconsciously.

The reprogramming away from a direct word-to-meaning connection to a sound-out-the-letters connection was the responsibility of the memory process administrator. You probably experienced some frustration on the part of this administrator when you first read the sentence. How long did it take your administrator to reprogram the way you read it? Were you able to sound out these "words"? How quickly did your reading of this sentence speed up? All of these reflect the working of different parts of Intelligent Memory. But however badly they started, they improved just from doing the exercise.

3. "Houston is Los Angeles with the climate of Calcutta." (Molly Ivins)

A. Got it instantly.	B. Took a few seconds.	C. What?

To find this analogy amusing, you had to activate an assortment of stored memories. You had to tap into memories about the cities—Los Angeles as vast, vibrant, and famous for its entertainment industry, and Calcutta as hot, crowded, and steamy. Living in a steam bath would erase much of the charm of any city. So if this is what Houston is like, it's a mixed blessing indeed. It may add a little bit to the humor to know Molly Ivins is a Texan.

Now that you're warmed up, you may better appreciate the following similar descriptions:

> Phoenix, Arizona: "An oasis of ugliness in the midst of a beautiful wasteland" (Edward Abbey).
> Washington, D.C.: "A city of Southern efficiency and Northern charm" (John F. Kennedy).

4. Consider the following facts:

> Steven is a college senior.
> Steven entered college at age fifteen.
> Steven got fifteen job offers.

- How would you characterize Steven's final GPA?

Poor
Mediocre
Good
Very Good
Excellent

A. Got it instantly.	B. Took a few seconds.	C. What?

The most likely answer, that Steven's final grade point average was excellent, required you to store the basic facts about Steven, to connect them with other memories about college, grades, and job hunting, and then draw a conclusion. The memories you had to tap into had to include an understanding of GPA (grade point average), the realization that fifteen is a very young age to enter college, and the knowledge that fifteen job offers is an exceptional number. You had to connect these memories to identify their common factor, which is that they indicate Steven is smart and so probably earned excellent grades.

CONNECTIONS

1. What do you see?

A.	B.	C.
Got it instantly.	Took a few seconds.	What?

Of course, neither the hand that you most likely see nor the apple that the hand is holding are in this picture. The "hand" is just a bunch of connected shapes and the "apple" is mostly empty space. Your Intelligent Memory creates them by making connections between patterns. You probably experienced this before with the Dalmatian. This pattern recognition—making connections between familiar shapes and, more generally, between ideas—is one of the most valuable and versatile qualities of Intelligent Memory. If this ability does not work well, then ideas do not get linked, networks do not get created, and activations cannot occur.

2. What do you see here?

A.	B.	C.
Got it instantly.	Took a few seconds.	What?

If you instantly recognized both the elephant and the back foot, your Intelligent Memory made a series of adept connections as well as judicial distinctions. However, if your Intelligent Memory did not deliver the answer, then your memory process administrator was alerted because of the delay. Your memory process administrator then steered your eyes around the image to find what had baffled your Intelligent Memory. That more detailed look may have let you see the human foot. This is typical of the way parts of Intelligent Memory and its memory process administrator interact. Your Intelligent Memory is usually first out of the gate in trying to solve a problem and produce an answer. If it succeeds, you may not even become aware of its success because you'll move to the next problem. If Intelligent Memory fails, then its memory process administrator is awakened and ordinary memory is hitched up to go looking for a solution.

3. "When politicians try to stay in the middle of the road, they get hit from both sides."

A.	B.	C.
Got it instantly.	Took a few seconds.	What?

This aphorism requires a number of layered connections. In this case, the connections link concepts about political positions—Left, Right, or Center—with positions on a road. The aphorism calls on an analogy to depict the danger of the center position—endangered from both sides, while those on either side have to worry about only one. Your Intelligent Memory would have used some of the same mechanisms to understand this political witticism as it did to understand the comments about Houston, Phoenix, and Washington, D.C.

4. Identify the odd word in this sequence: skyscraper, cathedral, temple, prayer.

A. Got it instantly.	B. Took a few seconds.	C. What?

"Skyscraper," "cathedral," and "temple" are all buildings, making "prayer" the odd word if your mind makes the building connection. Some people, however, may make religious connections and conclude that "skyscraper" is the odd word (to appreciate this best, start at the end of the list and work forward). The different answers stem from different sequences of connections. This shows how variations in Intelligent Memory connections can lead to an enormous number of divergent thoughts. Because the number of possible combinations increases exponentially as you add memories and connections to your Intelligent Memory, its power increases explosively as you store knowledge and experience.

5. Which of these word combinations are mismatched?

Bittersweet
Dry ice
Bitter snow

A. Got it instantly.	B. Took a few seconds.	C. What?

The answer, "bitter snow," is an example of concepts that are not linked for most people. "Bittersweet" and "dry ice" were once also incongruous concepts, but we've learned to link them together into one idea. There is no limit to the new combinations your Intelligent Memory can learn. Just as you once learned what "bittersweet" means, "bitter snow" may come to have meaning if we get more acid rain.

6. This illustration requires you to look beyond a normal image and extrapolate to a creative idea. Can you explain the concept being demon-

strated? *Hint:* The drawing is based on an ad that appeared in a men's magazine.

A.	B.	C.
Got it instantly.	Took a few seconds.	What?

The connections sparked here—related to sled dogs, snow, and the physical effort of pulling—are unusual enough to generate a creative concept: Normally, we let dogs pull sleds. Thus, the man pulling the sled for fun must be a superenergized man indeed. You had to know a great deal to make these connections and get the humor. If you got it immediately, then you are adept at making these connections, and also adept at appreciating their incongruity, which is what gives this illustration its punch.

7. Can you tell what this picture was meant to symbolize?

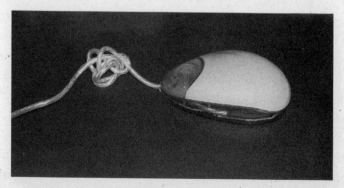

A.	B.	C.
Got it instantly.	Took a few seconds.	What?

This example too requires a creative leap. It's slightly more complicated than the previous picture because it illustrates a psychological concept, not a physical one, and so the leap must be farther. One part of the leap is from the mouse itself. The other is from the cord to the mouse, which is not smooth but a tangled knot. Clearly, it's a computer problem symbolized without words.

PROBLEM SOLVING

1. How quickly do you understand the meaning of the following?

- neurotica
- lipshtick
- "Only the mediocre are always at their best."
- "Are vegetarians allowed to eat animal crackers?"

A.	B.	C.
Got it instantly.	Took a few seconds.	What?

These words and expressions prompt a number of complex ideas. To understand them and appreciate their humor, your Intelligent Memory must quickly find distinctive pieces of information, especially concepts, and understand how they mesh. "Neurotica" and "lipshtick" were meant to be amusing titles for books. The humor in "neurotica" comes from the clashing memories evoked by "neurotic" and "erotica" (a Woody Allen sexual experience, perhaps). "Lipshtick" is a pun on "lipstick" meant to evoke "lip" in the sense of fast-talking (as in "Don't give me any lip") and "shtick," Yiddish for an entertaining routine or gimmick. *Lipshtick* is a book by a Jewish comedienne.

The statement about mediocrity tests your grammatical memories and your memory of the comparative degree of "best," which is a grade of goodness (good-better-best), and of the meaning of "mediocre," which is an absolute term, like "unique," that has no degrees. The statement about vegetarians draws on your knowledge of what vegetarians do and don't eat, your childhood appreciation for animal crackers (do you remember how much you thought they looked like animals?), and your experience with people of extreme beliefs. It pushes you to combine these and wonder whether committed non-meat-eaters could extend their beliefs to the point of ridiculousness.

2. What is the approximate temperature of Rio de Janeiro right now?

A.	B.	C.
Got it instantly.	Took a few seconds.	What?

If you know the exact answer and don't have to make an approximate estimation, this is not a good test of the Intelligent Memory we are trying to spark. The challenge for the Intelligent Memory here is to make a smart guess. If you made a good guess, then your Intelligent Memory dipped into your memories of geography and global weather patterns. You had to know that Rio de Janeiro is located in the Southern Hemisphere and that if you are in North America, the seasons in the two regions are reversed. Next, you had to retrieve memories related to precise temperature (perhaps you heard the day's temperature on the radio this morning) and roughly calculate an opposite temperature. Although you wouldn't be exact, you would be close enough for most purposes. (Check the weather map in the newspaper or the Weather Channel to see how accurate you were.) Lots of memories are activated here.

3. A man in a small town married twenty different women. All are still alive, he never divorced any of them, and he broke no laws. How did he do it?

A.	B.	C.
Got it instantly.	Took a few seconds.	What?

The key to understanding this apparent conundrum is remembering that there is more than one meaning for "married." The people who don't get this retrieve only the more common meaning. Their thinking starts with the idea of married as "united in matrimony." But "to marry" can also mean an act performed by members of the clergy or other officials. This meaning may have been more likely to come to mind if the puzzle had been about marrying a hundred people at once, but we wanted to keep it ambiguous. Once your Intelligent Memory locates the right meaning, the puzzle is solved: The man must be a minister or judge.

4. Can you identify this ink blot? How quickly?

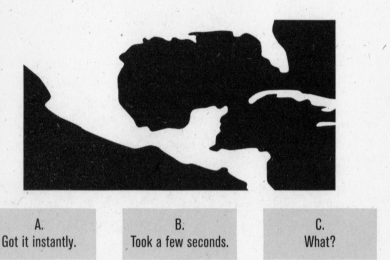

A.	B.	C.
Got it instantly.	Took a few seconds.	What?

This splotch is not the psychological phantasm we've come to expect from ink blots. Here's a clue: Think geography. Do you see the Gulf of Mexico, with Florida at the top right and Mexico and Central America curled under it?

You had to match this image to a geographic memory. It may have been challenging because it was rotated slightly counterclockwise compared to the way the Gulf region is usually depicted. So your Intelligent Memory had to try several different rotations, then find the right type of image to compare with this one. The clue that geography was some-how involved probably helped your search. Intelligent Memory can search through vast amounts of information, but finding the right memory is much quicker, and easier, if the search space can be narrowed with clues.

5. Follow this sequence. At what point do you see an identifiable object? (The page break is deliberate; don't turn the page until you've tried for a while.)

A.	B.	C.
Got it instantly.	Took a few seconds.	What?

If you saw a phone before the last three images, it was the result of your Intelligent Memory rapidly connecting lines and curves and matching the bigger chunks it created against mental pictures to find as a match a cordless telephone. This process was like the one that led to the Dalmatian identification except that here we gave different levels of difficulty—initially, far fewer visual clues—to tease out different levels of ability.

6. This cartoon depicts a visual pun. Do you know the expression that it alludes to?

A.	B.	C.
Got it instantly.	Took a few seconds.	What?

The answer is "Shuffle off to Buffalo." If you didn't get it, perhaps it isn't in your experience. It's the title of a famous old song from a 1930s musical (which has been revived so often that you don't have to be too old to know it). If you did get it, your Intelligent Memory had to be loose enough to find the sound similarities between the title of the song and the title of the cartoon. You also had to have enough sense of irony to appreciate the pun, helped perhaps by the knowledge that Buffalo is a very snowy place. You can understand the pun with Intelligent Memory without necessarily laughing at the joke. Puns and word games in general get their punch from the fact that they require retrieving memories from very disparate realms of knowledge, which is part of their charm.

MENTAL MISTAKES

1. Someone brings you an ancient coin in excellent condition. The coin is stamped "547 B.C."

- Is it likely to be a Greek or a Roman coin?

A. Got it instantly.	B. Took a few seconds.	C. What?

This question is a trick. It requires you to reexamine your first assumptions. Most people are likely to miss the implication of something being stamped with "B.C." (Before Christ). This designation is used only in historical hindsight and was never used contemporaneously, for how could someone know about the birth of Christ before it happened? Once you've tested your thinking for this flawed assumption, the answer becomes obvious: The coin is neither Greek nor Roman—it's a fake.

2. Sarah is single. She is in her thirties. She works as a vice president for a bank. In her spare time, she likes to attend lectures on women's issues.

- Which of these statement is more likely to be true?

Sarah is a vice president.
Sarah is a vice president and a feminist.

A. Got it instantly.	B. Took a few seconds.	C. What?

Here we need to consider which answer you gave and how fast you arrived at it. Most people will believe that it is more likely that Sarah is both a vice president and a feminist. They are wrong. If they came up with this answer quickly, the problem was in the automatic logic in their Intelligent Memory. If they came up with this after much thought, then the fault was in their conscious logic. Both can be helped, and applying probability logic will improve the one your Intelligent Memory uses.

It is a fact that Sarah is a vice president—that's what we are told. So the statement that "Sarah is a vice president" is 100 percent likely to be true.

Sarah *might* be a feminist. We don't know how likely that is, but we do know that we can't be 100 percent certain of it. The truthfulness of two statements taken together can never be more likely than the truthfulness of the less probable one. Since we can't be 100 percent certain that she is a feminist, the chance that she is both a vice president and a feminist must be less than 100 percent. That is why the first statement—"Sarah is a vice president"—is the correct answer.

Inferring from probabilities is one of the biggest challenges people face. Yet probabilities are all around us, and we have to know how to deal with them. By teaching yourself the correct logic in this case, you teach your Intelligent Memory the correct logic as well. The next time you see such a problem, you will be more likely to give the right answer automatically.

3. Students were given the following instructions: "Imagine a planet just like Earth existing somewhere in the universe. It is currently uninhabited. Your task is to design new creatures to inhabit the planet. Duplication of creatures now extinct or living on Earth is not permitted." The students were also shown sample creatures that had four legs, a tail, and antennae.

- Which of these two drawings do you think the teacher judged as more creative?

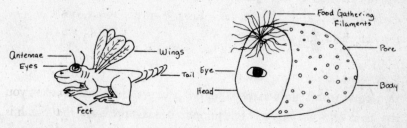

(Finke, Ronald and Thomas Ward, *Creative Cognition: Theory, Research, and Applications.* © 1992 Massachusetts Institute of Technology, The MIT Press.)

A.	B.	C.
Got it instantly.	Took a few seconds.	What?

The creature on the right is more creative because it shows less conformity to the samples mentioned in the question and more originality. The student who made the drawing on the left drew a design based on

Earth creatures. In contrast, the drawing on the right ignored conventional designs. The student took pieces he thought creatures everywhere might need, put them on a more unusual body, and combined them in a more unusual way. He formed unique connections.

4. Does this "word" and its "definition" make sense?

> *Bagonized:* How you feel while waiting for your luggage to come out of the baggage chute at the airport.

A.	B.	C.
Got it instantly.	Took a few seconds.	What?

Most of us have had this sensation. What makes "bagonized" amusing is the way it compresses an assortment of feelings into one word and therefore heightens the impact of the thought. By combining differing words and sounds, it creates a sudden *Pop!* of understanding. It's like a physical blow, with the impact concentrated rather than diffused. Even after the punch of "bagonized" is gone, it still affects your Intelligent Memory. Once-separate thoughts have now been condensed into one entry in your mind. This makes it easier to think about, move around mentally, and link with other thoughts.

5. A word rebus is a verbal puzzle that uses typography and the positioning of words and letters to suggest a larger meaning. For example, the rebus OHOLENE is "Hole in one," because the word "hole" is embedded within the word "one."

- Try to solve these rebuses:

1. SEARCH
   AND

2. TIMING
   TIM   ING

3. WEAR
    _____

    THERMAL

4. _____

    READ
    _____

5. HE'S/HIMSELF

A.	B.	C.
Got it instantly.	Took a few seconds.	What?

These puzzles are difficult. Your Intelligent Memory has to identify, sort, and test numerous memories to find the right matches. You need to search your memory for common expressions and metaphors, not individual words. Adding to the difficulty is the fact that your memory of the literal meanings of the words interferes with solving the puzzles. With enough looping backward and forward, and trying out possible answers, you may have solved them. The solutions are "search high and low," "split second timing," "thermal underwear," "read between the lines," and "he's beside himself."

YOUR SCORE

Now here's the fun part—discovering how you are already using Intelligent Memory and learning how you might improve it. Add up how many A's (Got it instantly), B's (Took a few seconds), and C's (What?) you had in each section, and write those numbers in the appropriate box on the score sheet below.

Attention

A. Got it instantly	B. Took a few seconds	C. What?

Scratch-Pad Memory

A. Got it instantly	B. Took a few seconds	C. What?

Memory Storage

A. Got it instantly	B. Took a few seconds	C. What?

Connections

A. Got it instantly	B. Took a few seconds	C. What?

Problem Solving

A. Got it instantly	B. Took a few seconds	C. What?

Mental Mistakes

A. Got it instantly	B. Took a few seconds	C. What?

Examine your scores. Note both your overall performance and your scores on each of the individual categories. It is useful to compare your scores from each section to determine which areas of Intelligent Memory you find easy and which areas you struggle with. This will give you an idea as to what parts of the Intelligent Memory you will want to improve as you move through the book.

You actually get two pieces of information from this quiz. Your score tells you how quickly you arrived at your answers. Quick answers, the "A's," came from Intelligent Memory—nothing else works that fast. If you didn't have many rapid answers, either you're not unleashing your Intelligent Memory or you need to build it up more.

The second thing to examine is your accuracy. It doesn't matter if an answer's fast if it's wrong. Generally, slower thinking is going to be more accurate. But if your quick Intelligent Memory was also almost as accurate, congratulations! It perceives, makes connections, and sorts through those connections well. If your rapid Intelligent Memory gave the wrong answers, then you need to find out what was wrong. Was the problem in your attention, scratch-pad memory, storing, connections, finding memories, or mental tuning? Again, look back on how you did in these sections. The remainder of this book focuses on how you can improve your thinking in each of these areas.

We have not given a specific scoring scale because there isn't one to give. Each skill is a partner in the overall process of developing Intelligent Memory, even though some can be better developed than others.

Nevertheless, there is good news here regardless of your score. As with the hidden picture of the Dalmatian, the simple acts of *trying* to answer these questions and learning the right answers have begun to educate your Intelligent Memory. They have slightly altered how you think about problems, prompting you to read more carefully, to be more flexible in considering answers, to trust your hunches more, or to pause before deciding on an answer. You've got a head start on the exercises in the coming chapters, which focus on each Intelligent Memory thinking skill tested here. By the end of this book, you'll be much better prepared to tackle not just these kinds of tests, but real-life puzzles and creative challenges as well.

CHAPTER 3

Improving Your Intelligent Memory

Even though you already have a great deal of Intelligent Memory and use it all the time, you can learn to make it work better. There are many ways to do this. First, you can make new connections, which is what happens whenever you try something new. You did this the first time you opened a letter using a pencil or whatever you had lying around other than a letter opener. Your Intelligent Memory blazed a new connection between what you needed to do and what you had available.

A second way to improve your Intelligent Memory is by making sure it finds connections you already have that are useful. It's always easier and faster to find an existing connection than to create a new one. A third way is to prune elements and connections that are wrong. Intelligent Memory absorbs experience so easily that a lot of what's in it is wrong, such as connections that shouldn't have been made or routes that go in the wrong direction. We have miniminds that are totally mistaken. These all need to be erased. You can also help this process in your Intelligent Memory by developing good overall thinking habits.

The whole process is somewhat like physical exercise in that you have to train the right "muscles." However, unlike much physical exercise, building up even a single muscle can be productive and fun.

Improving your Intelligent Memory means shifting your focus from rote memorization toward more productive, and even enjoyable, kinds of thinking. It's shedding some of the usual ways of thinking and learning new tricks to handle demanding situations. It's throwing out the old baggage of worrying about misplaced objects or people's names and pointing your mind toward solving annoying, even troublesome, everyday problems. It's preparing yourself to tackle the really difficult problems and creative challenges.

Like many skills, the mechanics of Intelligent Memory take time and effort to acquire. Practice them long enough and often enough, however, and the process gets easier, ultimately becoming as natural as tying your shoelaces. At first, learning the basics can feel awkward and progress may seem glacial. Yet if you start slowly and on a small scale, the foundation you lay will build on itself. Gradually the process becomes faster, easier, and stronger. With time, your Intelligent Memory will take bigger bites, digest them faster, produce more elaborate thoughts, and generate more powerful miniminds.

To help you understand what this entails and to make it easier to start, we've divided the process into seven steps. Of course, Intelligent Memory normally works as one operation, but some aspects of it are so distinctive that we can separate them. Each of these steps gets a full chapter of explanation, then, in chapter 11, we show you how your Intelligent Memory integrates them in addressing everyday situations. First, here is a brief overview of these steps.

ENHANCING ATTENTION

Paying attention is critical to absorbing information in the first place. Attention is also used by our minds to select what to think about. We have two kinds of attention: conscious and unconscious. Conscious attention can focus on only one thing at a time, whether it's a world event or a thought inside our heads. Unconscious attention is automatic. It perceives many things at once and can track multiple thoughts at the same time. You already know this "surveillance system" in its simplest form. It's what forces your conscious attention to focus on something moving even before you're fully aware of what it is. In its more educated form, it's what directed Sherlock Holmes's skills to what he needed to see about Watson. Learning to improve your attention will help you make memories. Reinforcing your attention with a better Intelligent Memory will help you detect what you need to, whether you're scanning a scene or examining your own thoughts.

EXPANDING SCRATCH-PAD MEMORY

Our memory uses a temporary "scratch pad." This is our most active memory—it's where we keep ideas at our mental fingertips and ready for use. It's also where we put brief memories, like remembering to ask a cashier for change in quarters so you can feed a parking meter. However, it imposes a major limitation on our thinking because most people can keep no more than seven thoughts active at once. Even the smartest or most educated are limited to no more than about nine thoughts at a time. We can't overcome this constraint directly, but we can multiply what each of those thoughts represents. Instead of putting nine $1 bills in our mental wallet, we can put in nine $10 bills. This way, you pack a great deal more into the same space.

STORING MORE MEMORIES

If you save your memories as isolated facts, they are often hard to recover, and finding one doesn't help you find others. But if you save facts linked together in meaningful ways, then you've created a network, which is far stronger than any of its parts. Once you locate a single fact or memory, you can jump to another. Conversely, if a single memory is weak, the others in the network can bolster it. As you expand your network of connections, which happens exponentially, your Intelligent Memory generates more ideas.

SPARKING CONNECTIONS

This step involves making new connections or reinvigorating those that have withered or become blocked. You can do this by pushing your Intelligent Memory's natural tendency to try to find connections between ideas.

SOLVING PROBLEMS

A problem can be anything from fixing a broken button to cloning a deceased pet to dealing with your in-laws. What these all have in common is a goal, which can be as clear as finding the answer to a math problem or as fuzzy as having a "good" vacation. Intelligent Memory helps solve these kinds of problems partly because of its talent for finding the appropriate connections and partly because it can look for many possible solutions at once. If you're having difficulty solving problems of any kind, your Intelligent Memory may need to be tuned.

WORKING CREATIVELY

Being creative, particularly in the arts, and solving problems are often viewed as quite different, but they use the Intelligent Memory toolbox in similar ways. The major difference is that creative, artistic thinking is usually open-ended: Its primary goal is to go where no one has gone before. However, creative thinking and problem solving are both accomplished by finding new connections in Intelligent Memory, which is creative in itself. (Have you ever replaced a broken shoelace with a sandwich bag tie?) For advanced creative thinking, however, new connections can, and should, be looser and jump further than those needed for most problem solving. And creative thinking also has to serve a purpose, even if only to entertain or beautify. In this way, it resembles problem solving, except that the standards for success are more flexible. As Andy Warhol observed (and practiced), "Art is what you can get away with."

PREVENTING MENTAL MISTAKES

The miniminds created in our Intelligent Memory work automatically and rapidly. But what if they're wrong? What if you have a minimind that believes that $1 + 1 = 3$? This can happen because miniminds soak up experience, and experience can be wrong. Even if you are corrected and now have a minimind that knows that $1 + 1 = 2$, the old minimind is still whispering its answer. This can slow you down or cause you to produce the wrong result. The solution is to either get things right the first time or to double-check your thoughts or conclusions early in the process, before a mistaken minimind can become too deeply rooted. This can be done by getting in the habit of being careful in your thinking and realizing that an idea can be wrong, unworkable, or trivial. By double-checking, you'll ensure that your Intelligent Memory is as smart as it can be. At the same time, you will not only be strengthening the mental tools you have but also developing a new set of tools to help with other "jobs." By practicing double-checking, you make these tools an automatic part of Intelligent Memory, which becomes sharper each time you use it.

In the chapters that follow, we'll tell you more about these aspects of Intelligent Memory and provide exercises for improving them.

CHAPTER 4

Enhancing Attention

So much information bombards our senses and so many thoughts bubble inside our minds that we have developed automatic shields to protect ourselves from "information overload." As you read this, do you feel the chair you're sitting in? Do you see what's going on outside the window? Do you hear all of what's going on around you? Most likely you don't, because of these shields. Your conscious attention is not only the spotlight that you direct at what you're focusing on, it is also the door that keeps information out or lets it in. It filters your thoughts and keeps random ideas from encroaching on the main path of your thoughts.

This filtering comes at a price, however. You can't remember what it doesn't let in. So one of the most common causes of memory problems—in both Intelligent Memory and ordinary memory—is the exclusion of information because you haven't paid attention to it; your shield has kept it out. Paying attention means focusing when you should and resisting the distractions that prevent that focus. By focusing your attention, you engage your Intelligent Memory, which in turns enhances both your conscious attention and your automatic attention filters.

FOCUSING

Focusing attention turns all of your mental energy to the job at hand and is a natural way of triggering the brain systems that make memories permanent. Without focused attention and the hardening of memories, ordinary memories are fragile and temporary. The difference is enormous. In a study of attention, students were asked to read paragraphs. Some were told they would be tested on the material and others were not. Those who had not been told they would later be tested remembered less than 10 percent of what they had read, while those who had been told about the test remembered more than 90 percent.

There are many circumstances in which it's almost impossible to focus your attention. When you first meet someone, focusing can be difficult because so much else is often going on. In a single instant you're trying to remember the individual as well as an arbitrary label such as "Nina" or "Ralph," figure out how they relate to you, and determine whether you should care, or seem to care for the sake of someone you know. You may also be looking around the room for other people or thinking about what to do next. All these thoughts shift your mental spotlight away from remembering that Nina is the name of the person who is standing in front of you. No wonder you won't be able to remember what's-her-name. In truth, forgetting is expected because you never really knew who Nina was in the first place.

The benefits of focusing are much wider than simply remembering a name or specific thing. The neuronal energy used in focusing also triggers associations and solidifies related memories into a web that becomes part of our Intelligent Memory. For example, after being introduced to Nina and using her name a couple of times ("My husband has told me so much about you, Nina"), you cause your focused attention to stir a memory of what your husband said earlier ("She has a darkroom in her basement") and of an article about famous women photographers, all sparking the idea that she might know where you could find a photo you've been looking for. Now, at some point in the future "Nina" has a chance of coming to mind when you think about things photographic.

People usually don't focus because they're rushed, bored, or distracted. They feel they don't have the time. However, if what you need to remember is important, it's a waste of time *not* to focus. Medical school is notorious for demanding memorization of reams of uninteresting, unconnected facts about parts of the body. For example, the part of the brain you use heavily for ordinary memory is the *hippocampus,* so named because it resembles the mythical seahorse (the forequarters of a horse, *hippos,* attached to the hindquarters of a fish). Now imagine remembering a thousand of these Latinate combinations as well as what they mean and where they're located.

When I was in medical school and trying to cram my memory with facts, I didn't do as well as I wanted. My roommate, however, not only studied less than I, but he also did much better on tests. When I finally overcame my pride and asked him his secret, he explained that he didn't want to spend any more of his time studying than he had to, so he forced himself to concentrate. By focusing his complete attention on what he had to learn, he could later reward himself with free time. It worked for him, and it worked for me once I applied the same strategy.

FAMILIARITY HELPS

Focusing attention is easier if you can match the new material you're trying to remember with something you've seen or heard before. It's easier to pay attention to something if there's already a place in your mind for that kind of information.

Experts absorb information quickly and thoroughly because they relate it to relevant memories they've already acquired. An expert in any field, whether it's chess, bridge, dancing, typing, music, sports, or collecting wine labels, has developed an attention so skilled and perceptive that it resembles intuition.

A classic experiment conducted in 1973 with master and novice chess players highlighted the abilities of expert attention. A chessboard was set up with 24 pieces on it, arranged just as if they had been positioned in the middle of a real game. Both groups of players looked at the board for five seconds. The players were then asked to reconstruct the exact location of as many pieces as they could recall. The masters and novices were also asked to look for five seconds at a chessboard with 24 pieces that had been placed randomly. The memories of both the experts and the beginners were the same for the pieces on the random board. However, when the board was set up like an actual game, the experts' memories far outstripped those of the novices. The experts remembered the positions of 16 of the pieces on the board, while the novices could remember the placement of only 4 of them.

This difference was attributed to the fact that the experts remembered the pieces in terms of patterns that were already very familiar to them. The less experienced novices didn't have these "reference" patterns in their minds for help. But, with the random board, pattern memory couldn't help, exposing the experts' raw ability to remember as being no better than average.

ATTENTION LAPSES

Many memory problems arise not from forgetting but from lapses of attention. By not focusing and instead sporadically tuning in and out, you remember only part of what's happening. You may in fact be doing it right now if your thoughts are drifting off to your dinner plans while you're reading. Everyone suffers from bouts of inattention or poor focus. Fatigue, hunger, and sleepiness can especially wreck havoc with our ability to focus. For some people, it pervades their daily mental lives.

Letting your mind wander can be fun, usually more fun than whatever you're doing at the moment. And if you're an artist, letting your mind wander may be part of your job. For most, though, it wastes time because we don't do or remember what we should, so we have to do it over or don't ever get it right.

Our minds wander more often than we think. Students in a Chicago high school provide an example. One of the classes was for high-achieving upperclassmen, and the teacher was one of the more popular in the school because of his interesting lectures. The lesson of the day was Chinese history and how the troops of Genghis Khan moved through the west of China, outflanking their adversaries along the Great Wall, then continuing north to conquer Yenching. During the lesson, a pager on the teacher's desk beeped at a random time, and the teacher asked the students to write down what they were thinking about at that moment.

The students' minds were elsewhere. Of the 27 in the class, only 2 were even remotely thinking about China. Most were thinking about lunch, the weekend, a boyfriend or girlfriend, or a sporting event. Of the 2 who were thinking about China, one was recalling a meal his family had at a Chinese restaurant the previous week and the other was wondering why Chinese men wore ponytails. Little Chinese history was remembered or learned in that 40 minutes.

This happens at the university level as well. Now that many lecture halls have been wired for Internet access, professors can find out whether students are reviewing the lecture notes or surfing elsewhere. In one class surveyed, over half of the students were elsewhere.

We're more susceptible to distraction when doing something routine—things we've done dozens of times before and assume we can do on autopilot. Unless we do a regular attention check while performing some activity, habit can take over and pretty soon our mind is off the subject. An airline pilot conducts an attention check when he reviews his list of instrument functions every time he flies. Although he's gone through the sequence many times before, he methodically avoids relying on habit and focuses on each step.

Inattention can get us into serious trouble. An expert driver—a stock-car racer, for example—has built up reflexive responses to emergencies through forethought, practice, and experience, so that even without conscious attention, these emergency miniminds jump into action when they detect the need. The skilled driver knows immediately to turn into a skid, as counterintuitive as that may be. However, those of us who are less skilled don't have these particular miniminds. In an emergency, our unskilled minimind tells us to turn away from the skid, which makes it worse. Paying attention and conscious thought can override this unskilled minimind and remind us of a better way to respond.

THE ATTENTION BOTTLENECK

Even focusing cannot overcome a basic limitation: conscious attention can handle only one thing at a time. We can keep just one thought in the spotlight of our mind at any moment. Although we may seem to do several things at once, we're really juggling them. We're keeping one in the spotlight briefly, then the next, and so forth until the turn for the first thought comes again. Even a computer is not really multitasking when it operates. It just seems to do so because it is so fast. Our brain machinery is about 100 million times slower than the computers sitting on our desks, and our one-thing-at-a-time attention is even slower. The teenager who talks on the phone while doing her physics homework may think she can listen to her girlfriend's problems and calculate formulas at the same time, but at any one moment, one of these activities has been pushed onto a back burner, waiting its turn.

Multitasking imposes two costs. One is direct: There is simply less mental time available for any single stream of thought. There is also an indirect cost: It takes time to put one thought aside and pick up another, and the little bit of forgetting that goes on during the process can weaken the thoughts. Anyone who's forgotten the beginning of a phone number while waiting to hear the end knows the toll of this forgetting. When we're multitasking, each thread of thought is getting much less attention than we think. If you undertake two activities, each receives less than 50 percent of your brain power.

Dramatic evidence of this comes from studies of oxygen use in the brain. In 2001, scientists at Carnegie Mellon University studied what happens to brain energy (in the form of oxygen) when someone does two complicated tasks at the same time. They first asked their subjects to listen to complex sentences, such as, "The pyramids were burial places and they are one of the seven wonders of the ancient world," and to say whether the statements were true or false. As they were listening and speaking, the subjects' brains were scanned using functional magnetic resonance imaging. Distinct areas of their brains lit up, indicating neuronal activity.

Next, the subjects were shown pairs of three-dimensional figures and asked to mentally rotate them and decide whether the pairs matched. Their brains were also scanned during this task. Different areas were activated during this task than those activated during the language-comprehension test. However, each task was about equally difficult, and each used approximately the same amount of oxygen.

Last, the students simultaneously rotated three-dimensional objects and listened to complex sentences. The resulting scans didn't show the brain using double the energy applied to a single task. It used far less. Thus, dividing attention didn't make the brain work harder, it just diluted the mental effort that could be applied to each task.

Dividing attention also reduces how much time and effort are devoted to solidifying memories. The thoughts and memories of someone switching between points of concentration can become as flawed as those of someone who's impaired by age, alcohol, or sleep deprivation. The hazards of multitasking are especially apparent when people use cell phones while driving. It's not the cell phone itself that causes the problem but the fact that the driver talks and thinks about what he's saying when he should be thinking about driving. Years ago, before the hazards of distracted driving were widely known, I was riding in a car with a famous cognitive scientist. He apologized profusely but refused to talk to me while he was driving. He knew only too well how it drained his driving ability.

Some activities don't require much mental oversight or don't have serious consequences if they go wrong. You can make dinner while talking on the phone, if you don't mind occasionally overcooking. And breaking up a boring routine with something different can help keep you on task overall. But multitasking raises the chances that something will go wrong or that you won't be able to shift your mind back quickly enough. So ask yourself before you undertake simultaneous activities: If something does go wrong, will the multitasking have been worth it? For burnt toast, the answer is probably yes. For a car accident, probably not.

Of course, no one's going to stop multitasking or dividing their attention. So the most practical approach is to decide which task needs more attention and accept an imperfect performance on the lesser task(s). Similarly, it's helpful to know that the act of switching attention requires energy and effort and reduces the total amount of mental energy you apply. Multitasking is more tiring than focused attention. As a result, you may not be able to spend the same length of time multitasking as you can focusing on a single subject.

The more someone becomes experienced in juggling a particular task, which is what happens with driving, the easier it is to load on another mental job. You'll find it more efficient to switch between familiar tasks that require low energy than to flip back and forth between novel tasks. Some experts also recommend setting a time limit for a certain task and using an alarm to remind you to switch. If you're online sorting through e-mail and also handwriting a memo, you may set a timer to ring every few minutes to help you shift attention. When astronaut Jerry Linenger was on the space station Mir and handling lots of tasks, he wore three or four watches set with different alarms so that he was reminded to switch tasks.

AUTOMATIC ATTENTION

Given the limitations of conscious attention, we're fortunate that we have another more comprehensive attention system working for us: automatic attention. Automatic attention is what monitors the sights, sounds, touches, smells, tastes, and internal sensations that constantly bombard us. It is a part of our Intelligent Memory that works quickly and before conscious thought. Automatic attention is what turns your eyes to a speck moving on the floor long before you're aware of what you're doing or before you realize there are ants in the kitchen. Automatic attention monitors everything we're exposed to and also monitors our thoughts. It doesn't require mental energy; it's a self-contained, separate auxiliary system for our thoughts and memories.

We're largely unaware of the information automatic attention delivers. The thoughts accompanying it are generally shallow and superficial, and the memory it produces tends to be insubstantial—little more than a short film clip or sound bite. This kind of attention can impart feelings of familiarity or a sense of knowing without providing details to fill in blanks. It's often a source of indistinct feeling, like a hunch, an instinct, or a vague sense of dread. Even though it gives us relatively little indication of its efforts, automatic attention is constantly working and on the lookout for anything that may be important to us. How it decides what's important is determined by our Intelligent Memory.

Automatic attention is what a practiced driver uses for most things she has to do. She responds to stop signs, avoids potholes, and makes all the tiny adjustments necessary to keep a car going without giving it a thought. When we're just beginning to drive, we're acutely aware of the mental effort it takes to pay attention to all the tasks and of how this awareness does not pick up everything. We don't know how to deal with potholes, balls in the street, children in crosswalks, stop signs, and other drivers all at once. That's because we haven't yet formed the Intelligent Memory that produces automatic attention, so we're stuck with our conscious attention, which is frequently overwhelmed by all it has to deal with.

After repeated attention to driving cues, however, the memories begin to stick, the miniminds develop, and unconscious, automatic attention takes over. Once your mind has learned how to recognize everything you need to drive safely, your attention to driving can switch from conscious to largely automatic. For experienced drivers, the details of driving are handled by automatic attention and Intelligent Memory, which has the plans for handling typical situations. For example, automatic attention handles the routine driving chores and also tells you that a cat has dashed in front of the car. Conscious attention can then take over to check the rearview mirror for a tailgater before it lets your Intelligent Memory slam the brakes. Your mind isn't completely on automatic—it's still prepared for the unexpected and watches to make sure nothing goes wrong. That's why diverting attention can be so dangerous.

We can train this automatic attention to take over all sorts of tasks. Some people can type without thinking about the typing process, some can work a calculator without thinking about each action. The seasoned pedestrian can glide through slowly moving traffic paying very little attention. When we do something guided by automatic attention, we're constantly building on intelligent memories that, in turn, make us even more efficient. The skilled driver who moves to Minnesota and learns to drive on black ice has acquired a new set of memories that will forever make his driving that much better. As you become an expert at something, your memory becomes more intelligent. Sherlock Holmes's rapid appraisal of Watson on their first meeting was an example of automatic attention fueled by Intelligent Memory. The example was fictional, but the process is what every expert learns.

A few years ago our friend Martha was shopping for a used car and found a little red coupe she wanted to buy. This was her first venture into the world of used cars and, knowing that she might not pay attention to important features, she asked her friend Dan, an amateur race-car driver, to inspect the coupe. Dan began his inspection as she had, checking the odometer, scanning the engine for wear and tear, and looking underneath the carriage for telltale signs of bodywork. His sleuthing went much further than hers, though. He examined the accelerator and brake pedals to see if the condition of the rubber covering was consistent with the number of miles on the odometer. While her automatic attention had searched no further than the condition of the cloth seats, he combed through the mats and carpeting, where he found tiny shards of glass. These, he explained, were from a broken window and meant that the car may have been in an accident. Thus, she had to look for any shoddy repair work.

Dan's finely tuned unconscious attention was alerting him to what his mental scanners were finding. He wasn't doing it deliberately, but saw the small details because his knowledge and his experience had trained his vision to look for them. The slivers of glass were "visible" to Martha too but her attention didn't focus on them and their significance. Having found the slivers of glass, Dan was even more primed to look for other things that might have gone wrong in a collision. Since Dan looks at a lot of used cars, his Intelligent Memory is kept filled with examples that are important and potentially useful the next time he checks out an old car.

Automatic attention can be improved to a remarkable degree. The training that U.S. Marine snipers go through is an example. At a three-month-long sniper school, Marines learn to observe tiny details and to commit them to memory. They learn not only to notice a discarded tin can but also to think about what it might mean—what it says about an enemy's food supply or morale or the size of an enemy force. This training starts on the conscious level, but the skills eventually become entrenched into unconscious and automatic attention.

Sniper school instructors regularly play a game called "Keep in Memory, Sniper," in which ten items are scattered about the floor of a room

while the students are distracted (shouted at, actually). They are expected
to pay attention during this process but are not directed toward anything
in particular. The students are then sent to a class or for a run. Hours
later, maybe even a day later, they're asked to draw each item that was on
the floor and give a description of its function, size, shape, color, and condition. Students have to get eight out of ten right to pass. In another exercise, small details in the students' surroundings are changed—a photo
in a gallery along a hallway might be replaced with another—and the students are asked what they've noticed. This training in observation and remembering gradually causes the skills to become so ingrained in the
students that performing them is automatic. No matter where they're de-
ployed, these Marines automatically deploy their unconscious attention.

Developing automatic attention isn't always work. Readers delighted
in trying to find the hidden name "Nina" in cartoonist Al Hirschfeld's
drawings for the *New York Times*. (Nina is his daughter.) Supposedly,
the U.S. Air Force has used hunts for "Nina" as an exercise for pilots
learning to spot targets.

Marine snipers must be aware of almost everything because, especially in a foreign environment, they don't know what's important and
what's not. Until they gather experience observing a situation, their attention is on wide alert. But part of the more routine learning process is
recognizing what you can ignore. We can't be mentally involved in
everything around us. We have to be selective, and our Intelligent Memory reminds us of what's germane. For example, read this paragraph:

Many foods cost too much. Food costs would diminish if
farm land was not so costly. In addition, tractors and additional tools cost way too much. Politicians should also
diminish any tax on farm products. A high tax on such products hurts us all.

Do you remember the main points? Probably, because reading for
meaning is what most people do. But did you notice that the letter "e"
never appeared? Most likely you didn't, because something like that
wouldn't be important to you, and most of the time, you'd be right.

Learning what to observe carefully and what to ignore comes from repetition, trial and error, and instructing our conscious attention to hold on to memories of sights and sounds that might be useful later. If you were to read something that sounded slightly peculiar, you'd probably be alerted to look for a trick, and you'd notice quirky features. For instance, notice anything about this list of words?

The
Red
Impala
Can
Kick
You

You probably thought these words had a bizarre meaning while also noticing that the first letters spell TRICKY. If you were a spy learning code, this may be an important form of attention. Otherwise, you've slightly sharpened your attention but also know that what you detected is relatively unimportant.

In the same way, we learn to attend to what is important. The cook pays attention to whether the butter in the pastry dough is cold enough because that determines whether the pie crust will be flaky. The car mechanic listens to the way a car starts because that determines whether he needs to check the spark plugs. The psychiatrist watches a patient's body language because that tells him if she's angry. Everyone possesses an automatic attention scanner for certain things. And with effort and practice, you can extend your attention skills, both automatic and conscious, so that you create a sensitive set of eyes and ears for your Intelligent Memory.

The "cocktail party effect" is an example of all the parts working together. Imagine standing in a room full of people talking, the sounds of many conversations reaching your ears. You're talking to the person in front of you. Yet even though you are engaged in conversation, your ears pick up other sounds in the room, especially familiar words, like the name of a favorite baseball team or someone saying your name. While you're focused on the person you're talking with, stashing away what you want to remember, your unconscious attention is scanning the room for sounds that match familiar memories. Hearing them, you try to understand better by revving up the mental circuits to deal with that part of the room and those particular topics.

EXERCISES

These exercises ask you to flex both your conscious and automatic attention as you read or look at a picture. What you notice or overlook provides an indication of your strengths in verbal and visual attention. Of course, you have other forms of attention, such as those for movement or smells, but these can't be exercised in a book. Be sure to complete the exercise, answering the questions, before reading the explanation.

1. Whom do you see in this picture?

(Cecil Stoughton, White House/John Fitzgerald Kennedy Library, Boston)

Explanation: On the right side, just short of the midpoint from the bottom, is John F. Kennedy. This exercises your automatic attention, which rapidly scans for a familiar face without your being aware of the process.

2. Read the following, then cover it up and answer the question:

> "Please accept my ressignation. I don't want to belong to any club that will except me as a member." (Groucho Marx)

- Did you notice any mistakes in the quote?

Explanation: There are two errors. "Resignation" is misspelled and "except" is the wrong word; "accept" is correct. While this piece flexes your reading attention, it also exercises your ability to sort relevant from irrelevant information. You're asked to cover the passage after reading it so that you're forced to recall details and decide which matter.

3. Read the following, then cover it up and answer the questions:

> You are the driver of a bus that can hold a total of 72 passengers (there are 36 seats that can hold 2 passengers each). At the first stop, 7 people get on the bus. At the next stop, 3 people get off and 5 get on. At the next stop, 4 people get off and 2 get on. During each of the next two stops, 3 passengers get off and 2 get on. At the next stop, 5 passengers get off and 7 get on. When the bus arrives at the next to the last stop, 2 people get on and 5 get off.

- How many stops did the bus make?
- What was the name of the driver?

Explanation: This exercise also requires you to sort through relevant and irrelevant details. To answer it correctly, you need to discard the deliberately confusing numbers and recall the beginning, which stated that the driver is "you."

4. Take about five seconds to read each of the following phrases, then cover them up and write them down as you remember them.

PARIS
IN THE
THE SPRING

ONCE
IN A
A LIFETIME

BIRD
IN THE
THE HAND

Explanation: In each phrase, an article is repeated. If you didn't see that, you were reading on automatic. You saw the phrases, felt familiar with them, and so let your mind wander to something else.

5. What do you notice in this picture?

(Elliott Erwitt, Magnum Photos)

Explanation: You saw the cute dog, but did you also notice the legs of the larger dog on the left? The difference in scale and your expectations—you'd expect four legs on a dog—may have led you to misperceive the larger dog's legs as those of another human. Your mind may have done a double-take as it realized the mistake and looked again. This exercise requires you to monitor what your eyes pick up and make sure nothing is missed.

6. Read this paragraph, then answer the question:

By ensuring consistency in the development and integration of process plans, you will facilitate the management processes to develop implementation plans for the processes they manage. You will also be business plan modeling, rolling plan methodologies and the measurement of process effectiveness. As Integration Planner, your position will be at the interface of the personal, planning and implementation and measurement matrix.

■ What's the job that's being described?

Explanation: This is an advertisement for a job that appeared on the Internet, though we don't know what kind of job. If you are the rare person who understood it, then you are probably a motivated reader. Only a highly involved reader, such as the person who wrote the piece or an employee who encountered it in a memo from a boss, would take the effort to decipher it.

7. What strikes you about this picture?

(Elliott Erwitt, Magnum Photos)

Explanation: We have a good idea what got your attention, but there should be another point of focus: the model (although some people are more distracted by the students' socks). The contrast between our expectations of an artist's model, who should be the naked one in an art class, and this scene, makes it a funny picture.

8. Look at this block of randomly positioned letters. As you're scanning, draw a line through as many Ts as possible in 30 seconds.

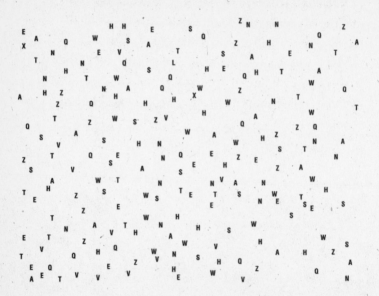

Explanation: There are twenty Ts in this exercise. To find them, you probably moved your attention and eye rapidly over the figure, taking only enough time on each letter to determine if there was a match. When you found a possible match, you looked more closely. Only then did your attentional filter decide that what you were seeing was a T. Scanning—starting with a quick decision, then honing in to make a finer distinction—is an effective way of using attention if you have an inkling of what you're looking for.

9. Read the following and note your reaction:

Seconds later, a silky voice answered, and I told her what was on my mind. "I understand you can help me set up an hour of good chat," I said.

"Sure, honey. What do you have in mind?"

"I'd like to discuss Melville."

"Moby Dick or the shorter novels?"

"What's the difference?"

"The price. That's all. Symbolism's extra."

"What'll it run me."

"Fifty, maybe a hundred for Moby Dick. You want a comparative discussion—Melville and Hawthorne? That could be arranged for a hundred."

"The dough's fine," I told her and gave her the number of a room at the Plaza.

"You want a blonde or a brunette?"

"Surprise me," I said and hung up. Hardly an hour had passed before there was a knock.

"Hi, I'm Sherry."

They really knew how to appeal to your fantasies—long straight hair, leather bag, silver earrings, no make-up.

She lit a cigarette and got right to it. "I think we could start by approaching Billy Budd as Melville's justification of the ways of God to man, n'est-ce pas?"

"Interesting, though not in a Miltonian sense." I was bluffing. I wanted to see if she'd go for it.

Explanation: This excerpt from Woody Allen's "The Whore of Mensa" may have stirred your reading attention in a number of ways. If you have a literary bent, you attended to the idea of English-lit-for-pay and were amused by the notion that someone would ask for a hundred dollars to talk Melville. You may have been entertained by another point of focus, namely the allusions to a sexual rather than a literary exchange. Whatever caught your attention here was sparked by your Intelligent Memory.

Attention is the first step on the way to forming Intelligent Memory. The ideas and impressions must next be packaged—that is, organized—and stored in long-term memory. Intelligent Memory depends on a deep and permanent repository, and building one requires a host of storage strategies, as you'll read in the next chapter.

CHAPTER 5

Expanding Scratch-Pad Memory

HOW GOOD IS YOUR SCRATCH-PAD MEMORY?

There was a strong noise emanating from the dark house. Bob had to venture in to find out what was there. He was terrified: Rumor had it that the house was haunted. He would feel more secure with a stick to defend himself and so he went and looked among his baseball equipment. He found a bat that was very large and brown and was flying back and forth in the gloomy room. Now he didn't need to be afraid any longer.

Working memory, also known as scratch-pad memory, is essential for understanding this story. The story is a bit jarring because it deliberately puts the image of a baseball bat into your working memory, then abruptly changes that image to something "brown and . . . flying back and forth." For a few moments, your working memory was fixed on the notion of a baseball bat, until it was corrected.

Working memory is the intermediate stage between paying attention and long-term memory storage. It's the temporary scratch pad on which everything that might get committed to memory is first managed—a short-term holding place for memories while your mind organizes and sorts through them. Nothing gets into your permanent memory, including ordinary memories and all the memories that form your Intelligent Memory, without first going through scratch-pad memory.

This memory function is also called "working" memory because it's where the work of memory goes on. Here is where you keep the first part of what you're hearing or reading so you can understand the last part. It's your Post-it note for things you have to remember for at least a little while before deciding whether to keep them. It's the spot for making mental notes while figuring out the best route to the hardware store or the best solution to your child's math problem. Its work is managing both the information that may come into memory from outside and the information coming from your inactive memory storage space and moving into active focus.

If you understood the story at the beginning of the chapter, you have a good-sized working memory. Many people don't understand the story because it packs in too much information for their working memories. To understand the twist at the end, you have to remember all of the facts that came before it, and not many people have a large enough working memory to do that.

Despite its critical position on the route into our memory network, working memory has severe limits. The scratch pad is fairly small and limits how many thoughts you can actively juggle in your mind at one time, how much you can funnel into your long-term memory, and how many memories you can retrieve from your permanent memory at once. Because working memory imposes such limits, anything we can do to build it up has major implications for all our memory abilities, including Intelligent Memory. In this chapter we'll show you how to overcome scratch-pad memory's limitations and harness it to your Intelligent Memory. First, a few more checks of your working memory.

WORD RECALL TEST

Read each sentence that follows, then cover them all up.

The produce man sold many apples and oranges.
The sailor had been around the world several times.

The house had large windows and a massive mahogany
   door.
The bookseller crossed the room, scowled, and threw the
   manuscript on the chair.

Once you have covered them, try to recall the last word in each sentence. If you can remember the last word in every sentence, you have an excellent working memory for words. This is a good predictor of your ability to understand what you read. University students who did well on this test were also good at reading comprehension. They understood complicated passages more quickly and accurately than students with a small working memory for words.

DIGIT SPAN TEST

If you suspect your memory for numbers is better than that for words, take this digit span test. The best way is to have someone read it to you instead of reading it yourself. This is because the kind of memory being tested has a strong auditory component. The tester should read each line of numbers, pause, then ask you to repeat them. The tester should also keep track of the ones you get right.

3—4—7: Pause, test.
8—1—6—5—7: Pause, test.
3—1—6—8—9—2—4—7: Pause, test.
5—9—6—3—2—1—7—4—8—6—2—9—3—4: Pause, test.

The first and second lists of numbers were probably easy for you to recite. As the list grew longer, however, you surely struggled and found that by the time you heard the end of the list, the first number had vanished from your head. With the longest list, you might have recalled a couple of the early numbers and a couple of the last numbers but not the numbers in between. In all likelihood, you probably could not remember more than about seven numbers. That's the capacity of your working memory. Once at capacity, your mind has to push one number out to get another number in.

Working memory is essential for everything you do. Whether you're making coffee, writing a letter, figuring how much change you're owed, or solving a problem with your computer, you need working memory to remember what you've just done and what you plan to do next. Working memory is so basic to intelligent processing of information that every modern computer has it too. A computer's memory scratch pad is called random access memory, or RAM. RAM is where information is kept in its most active form, the one most quickly available. In the same way, working memory keeps information available at your mental fingertips—you don't have to take the time and effort to search your mind's hard drive to find it.

Even simple conversation is impossible without working memory. Our scratch pad enables us to hold words in our head until we can decipher what they mean. If you heard the following sentence (shown with two possible endings), you would not know what the speaker meant until you heard the last few words, then recalled the first words: "He strode across the court and protested to the judge that his opponent was breaking the rules by using (*an illegally strung tennis racquet*) (*inadmissible evidence*)."

Only when you hear one of the possible endings of the sentence can you understand whether the speaker is talking about a lawyer or a tennis player. You can do this because your scratch-pad memory was holding on to the words at the beginning of the sentence so that you could immediately refer back to them.

We really have many small memory scratch pads. For example, remembering conversation uses the one for sounds, particularly words. Another one you're probably familiar with is the scratch pad for visual images, which enables us to remember quick glances. These smaller scratch pads are all part of our working memory system and have the same limitations.

Even with all the little scratch pads pulling together, working memory can manage only a limited amount. As mentioned earlier, for most people this is about seven items at any one time—it normally ranges from as few as five to as many as nine. This limited number of items is constant whether you're trying to remember words, numbers, sights, sounds, symbols, or ideas.

There is bad news, good news, and better news in this.

First, the bad news: The limit on working memory applies to everyone and it applies to everything. The psychologist who first identified this feature of our memory system, George Miller, looked at dozens of studies that seemed to put relatively few demands on memory. For example, people were asked to listen to sounds and identify as many separate ones as possible or to tell how many different concentrations of salt they were tasting. But they were all memory tests too, since people had to remember what they had heard or tasted to tell whether they remembered something different.

Regardless of whether the findings concerned tones or tastes, they were always the same. Listeners could easily pick out two or three tones, but as they thought they heard more, their mistakes increased. Ultimately, the listeners could hear, without error, only six distinct pitches. Other people, asked to distinguish between levels of loudness, could identify no more than five at a time. Those tasting different concentrations of salt in water could tell no more than four apart without error. People were also tested to see how many playing cards they could identify in a single glance. The number always hovered around seven. No matter what country, what language, or what test, this limit kept appearing.

Miller concluded: "We possess a finite and rather small capacity for making such unidirectional judgments and this capacity does not vary a great deal from one simple sensory attribute to another." He labeled this average capacity "the magical number seven." Miller noted that the idea that our minds are especially attuned to sevens is not new: "What about the seven wonders of the world, the seven seas, the seven deadly sins, the seven daughters of Atlas in the Pleiades, the seven ages of man, the seven levels of hell, the seven primary colors, the seven notes of the musical scale, the seven days of the week. . . ." Since ancient times, man has been connected with the number seven. One reason may be that it's the most our minds can grasp at any one moment. It's the capacity of our working memory.

There is some good that comes from this smallish working memory. It forces us to throw away memories not worth keeping. Imagine what your mind would be like if it remembered all the little things that flit in and out of your working memory. Without forgetting, we would be mired in mounds of trivial facts and impressions. Our minds would be a "junk heap of impressions." This is how a Russian psychologist described the mind of Solomon Shereshevskii, who remembered every number, word, and sensory experience he ever heard or saw. He remembered events from his infancy as readily as something he encountered days earlier. He could commit to memory a 50-digit number in less than two minutes and then, if asked fifteen years later to recall the number, could do it flawlessly. Not surprisingly, Shereshevskii spent years of his later life trying to forget the jumble of useless memories in his head.

CHUNKING

The good news to come from the discovery of the limits of working memory is that there is a way around it—chunking. We can't learn to hold more than an average of seven pieces of information at a time, but we can make the pieces themselves larger. It's like money—your purse can hold seven coins, but those coins can be pennies or silver dollars. You can remember no more than seven single-digit numbers at a time, but you can also remember seven five-digit numbers at once. Seven letters. Seven words. Seven sentences. Seven paragraphs. Seven chapters. Seven books. How? By chunking.

We naturally chunk when we learn how to speak and read. As we learn a language, we organize pieces of it—that is, sounds—into larger ones. A child learning to read begins with individual letters that are then clustered into syllables and words. Soon a working memory of seven words becomes a memory of seven sentences, and can, after long practice, grow into a memory of seven paragraphs. Through organization and packaging, we can outsmart the seven-item limit.

S.F., a college student, is a dramatic example of this. Researchers chose to study him because he was an average student with unexceptional scores on memory tests and college entrance exams. Unknown to the experimenters, he was a passionate cross-country runner and an enthusiastic member of the school's track team. At the beginning of the experiment, S.F.'s recall of a list of numbers was unremarkable. Like the other students in the study, after five days of hearing and reciting numbers, he felt he had hit his limit at eight numbers. Nevertheless, the experiment continued.

Then an amazing thing happened. The number of digits he retained after each list began to increase. And the number kept rising. By day 39 of the experiment, S.F. could recite a string of 22 digits. By the eightieth day, he was up to about 70 digits.

On his own, S.F. had devised a way to remember clusters of numbers rather than individual ones. Using his experience with track and cross-country running, he converted strings of numbers into running times. For instance, in his mind the numbers 3—4—9—2 became 3:49.2—a near world-record mile time. The four numbers merged into a single piece of information, giving his working memory room to hold six other clusters of numbers. S.F. created different categories of running times to allow for longer and longer strings of numbers. By the end of the experiment and more than 250 hours of training, S.F. had expanded his original digit memory from eight to more than eighty numbers. This improvement wasn't because he had increased the size of his working memory; he still could remember only seven or eight items. What S.F. did was chunk information so more could fit into each of the seven positions in his working memory.

We all chunk unconsciously. We learned to chunk so long ago that it feels like a natural part of thinking. Our minds like shortcuts, especially bits of information that can be clumped together and so require less effort to remember. For instance, you probably find these groups of letters easy to understand and remember: TV, IBM, TWA, USSR.

However, when you encounter the same letters in different groupings—IW, BMV, SRU, SATT—comprehension and remembering is much slower.

We readily chunk numbers, lumping them together in a variety of meaningful patterns. The phone number 212-3456 is easy to remember because it's in a sequence. The locker combination 9 right, 11 left, 10 right is easy to remember because, except for the inverted last two numbers, it's a famous date. Probably everyone has a personal way of lumping numbers together in order to make them meaningful and easy to remember. While S.F. used his personal knowledge of running times, other common hooks are birth dates, famous dates in history, and significant times of day.

In addition to learning to chunk for speaking and reading, we learn to chunk cultural information, like common symbols. A red circle with a line through it is a single chunk meaning "this activity is forbidden or illegal." There are also motor or procedural chunks: Most of us do certain things as a single activity, such as tying shoelaces or peeling an orange.

Chunking is one reason why experts of all kinds seem to know so much and have huge memories. Whether they're expert at cards, computer programming, or Italian cooking, their knowledge of their field is contained in huge chunks. And the more they practice their expertise, the larger their chunks grow. If someone is good at stud poker, for instance, and is dealt a hand with a nine of diamonds in the hole and eight of hearts, ten of diamonds, and seven of spades face up, he can see and think of the hand as a single piece of meaningful information—that is, a hand worth betting on. A novice card player has to think about this hand as four separate chunks, making it that much harder to think about how much wagering it merits.

Not all chunking happens naturally. At times, pieces of information don't have an obvious pattern or suggest something meaningful. Each item on a shopping list may appear to be quite separate and bear little relation to each other. More often than not, successful chunking requires thoughtful analysis. You have to search your memory for hidden characteristics that can bind bits of information together. There are countless ways to cluster information, from superficial qualities like a visual pattern, such as a common color or shape, or an auditory pattern, like a rhyme (which is why rhymes are easy to remember) to obscure features, like a historical connection.

The chunking that leverages scratch-pad memory and helps you acquire knowledge that you can convert to Intelligent Memory may take more effort than the chunking you need to remember phone numbers or shopping lists. This chunking is used to organize and remember complicated ideas and mental processes. One example is the chunking that takes numerous pieces of a problem and assembles them into a solution that is remembered and applied to future problems.

MAKING TIGHT CHUNKS

Chunks can be "loose" or "tight," depending on the relationship between the pieces. With loose chunks, the relationship is vague and may be a stretch. Medical students studying for exams use loose chunks to remember anatomy when they use an acronym made up of initial letters to remember lists of complicated parts. One such med student chunk is GET SMASH'D—the causes of sudden inflammation of the pancreas, namely *G*allstones, *E*thanol, *T*rauma, *S*teroids, *M*umps, *A*utoimmune, *S*corpion bites, *H*yperlipidemia, and *D*rugs.

Tying things together because they share an initial letter can be tenuous because often the way something is spelled bears little relationship to what it means, what it does, or other more important features. Medical students remember their loose chunks only if they have to repeatedly use the information when they practice. Otherwise, the information fades.

A better way to remember is to use more meaningful, "tighter," methods of chunking. Tight chunks contain pieces of information that are related in more than appearance—for instance, in function or importance, such as the process you go through to brush your teeth. Tight chunks are easier to remember, although sometimes harder to come up with and requiring more attention. The pieces of information may need to be picked apart to find common, meaningful shared qualities.

EXPLORING POSSIBLE PATTERNS

Many varieties of patterns can be discovered in a body of information. Of course, there are the obvious patterns that our eyes pick up immediately, like shape, color, size, or texture. Patterns that reflect the significance of different pieces of information are easier to remember. Chess players remember many varied opening moves not because the moves themselves are similar but because of their significance to the outcome of the game: Certain opening conventions in chess produce better results than others.

Ever wonder how good waiters can listen to a jumble of orders and substitutions and last-minute changes, then miraculously appear at your table with all the correct meals and hand them to the right people? By chunking according to a pattern. Researchers learned this by studying a group of waiters, including J.C., who was known to remember up to twenty complete dinner orders at one time. To find out how he performed this feat, the researchers constructed an artificial restaurant in their lab that offered eight meat entrées, five ways the meat could be cooked (rare to well done), five salad dressings, and three vegetables. The "restaurant" contained tables that could seat between two and eight people. All told, there were more than 600 possible order combinations that J.C. might have to remember.

J.C. and the other waiters took orders from a number of "patrons," but J.C. was the only waiter to remember them all flawlessly. He did this by chunking and labeling. Instead of trying to remember a string of separate orders, each containing an entrée, a salad dressing, and a vegetable, J.C. grouped the orders. For each table, he grouped together entrées, salad dressings, and vegetables, then attached a label or pattern to the group. For instance, he assigned degrees of meat doneness a number—1 for rare, up to 5 for well done—then remembered the string of numbers. If the four people at the table ordered their meat rare, medium rare, medium well, and rare, he thought of it as 1-2-4-1. He turned each selection of salad dressing into a letter, so that blue cheese became "B," oil and vinegar "O," and Thousand Island "T." The four diners asked for blue cheese, two oil and vinegars, and Thousand Island, which became "B-O-O-T."

J.C. extended his working memory to at least twenty items by creating a series of patterns meaningful to him. Here are other methods he could have applied to extend his working memory capacity:

- Use linking information for lists like instructions, such as a sequence of activities in which the last action in one step suggests the next.
- Use visual patterns such as color, texture, size, or position in space.
- Use letter, word, or numerical patterns, such as repeated pairs of letters, initial letters, word endings, or different combinations of numbers that always add up to the same total.

REASSEMBLING FOR MEANING

Patterns are everywhere, and the most useful ones are meaningful. They not only help you extend your memory, but also extend how well your mind thinks the next time you encounter the same kind of problem.

Years ago, a schoolteacher posed a problem for his class of ten-year-olds. He asked them to find the sum of all the numbers from one to one hundred (that is, $1 + 2 + 3 + \ldots + 98 + 99 + 100$). The teacher expected the students to be a long time working this out, but he had not even finished explaining the problem when one student handed in an answer. The teacher waited until the rest of the class finished, then compared all the answers. Only the quick student got the answer right, because he saw a pattern in the way the numbers added up. They could be paired, so that the sum of each pair was 101: $1 + 100 = 101$, $2 + 99 = 101$, $3 + 98 = 101$, and so forth. There were fifty pairs of numbers from 1 to 100, so 50 times 101, or 5,050, was the answer.

If you didn't see this pattern, don't feel bad. The ten-year-old was mathematical prodigy Carl Frederich Gauss, who grew up to be one of the greatest mathematicians of all time. But now that he showed the way, our memories can make it easier for us the next time. What's the sum of all the numbers from 1 to 99? You don't have to work this out from scratch; it's the sum of all the numbers from 1 to 100 that you already know (5,050), minus the extra 100, or 4,950.

FINDING MODELS

Sometimes it's easier to remember something as a process or a mechanism. By remembering as a single solution the individual steps you took to solve a problem, you have a "solution chunk" in your Intelligent Memory to use when you encounter a similar problem in the future. This method vastly increases the power of our thinking, since many problems are generic—you encounter the same problem over and over, just in different circumstances and different disguises. Investment problems, distance-rate-time problems, cost-benefit problems, and percentage problems regularly crop up in daily life. If you learn to appreciate the general problem lurking in the specifics, then not only will you remember the problem, you'll remember its solution.

For example, many people regularly encounter problems or decisions that can be chunked under the general category of "sunk-cost" problems. Here are some typical examples:

> A week after making expensive repairs on your car, replacing the ignition system, brake pads, and shock absorbers, you learn that it needs a new transmission. In deciding whether to invest more money in the car or get rid of it, you consider what you've already invested or sunk into it.

> Your shares of Skyrocket Corporation have dipped from the $20 each you paid to $10 each. In deciding whether to sell or not, you consider the amount of your initial investment.

But it's fruitless to consider the investment on the basis of how much you've already put in. It's much better to consider its future value. If buying a new transmission is going to give you a car that runs well for another five years, it will be worth it. If you think Skyrocket Corporation is going to do well next year, the stock will be worth holding. How much you've invested doesn't count—the sunk cost is down the drain.

Learning solutions this way creates problem-solving miniminds, ready to jump into action when circumstances are right. All their actions have been chunked together and function on automatic. You probably already have a number of problem-solving miniminds. To use them most effectively, you have to chop the problems down to size until your miniminds can tackle them. One way to do so is the work-backward method. You tackle a problem by understanding the goal and figuring what steps are needed to get there. Closely related is the means-ends method, which uses a series of subgoals; rather than working toward an ultimate solution, you solve a series of smaller problems that, together, solve the larger one. Another method is hill climbing—you pick steps that get you closer to a solution even if they're not the final solution. If progress isn't apparent, you take a step back and do something else that will move you closer. With practice and repeated experience solving problems, you can turn each of these methods into a single process you will try automatically, rather than a sequence of separate steps.

Chunking is an effective way of strengthening and developing your memory. As you'll read in the next chapter, there are numerous other strategies for saving memories so that you can get to them whenever you like, especially when you need Intelligent Memory.

EXERCISES

1. This exercise asks you to flex your scratch-pad memory. Read this paragraph, cover it up, then answer the question.

> Sitting with Bob, Paul, Rob, and the rest of my gang in the
> Grill yesterday, I began to feel uneasy. Jake had put a quarter
> in the jukebox. It was blaring one of the latest Christian rap
> favorites. I was studying, in horror, the reactions of my
> friends to the music. I was especially perturbed by the ex-

pression on my best friend's face. John looked intense and was pounding the table furiously to the beat. Now, I like most of the things other teenage boys like. I like girls with blonde hair, girls with dark curly hair, in fact, all girls. I like milkshakes, football games, and beach parties. I like jeans, t-shirts and Skechers. It is not that I dislike rap, but I think it shouldn't be taken too seriously. And here he was, all serious and tripping out over the music.

- Who was all serious and tripping out over the music?

Answer: John was wrapped up in the music. If you got this question right, your scratch-pad memory organized the names and information in the paragraph to form a number of large chunks. Each chunk was more than a jumble of isolated facts: It was a cluster of related information, like an image of boys, and how they were reacting, and how their reactions were affecting the other boys. Particular words in the paragraph, like "Christian rap," probably sparked a large chunk consisting of images, associations, and interpretations. If you incorrectly answered this question, it's possible that you did not know what to keep in your working memory. The paragraph offers no clues as to what's important. Furthermore, the mention of Christian rap, an unusual kind of music, might have stuck in your working memory and interfered with your ability to remember more.

2. The following square consists of nine different numbers but has a unique, unifying quality: Any way you add up the numbers—horizontally, vertically, or diagonally—they always total fifteen. The exercise is to turn your memory of this square into a single chunk by devising a way to remember the order of the numbers. While chunks of numbers can be dull and readily forgotten, chunks formed from more interesting information are better remembered, for instance, "For nine to free five, seven ate one six." The numbers can also be chunked crosswise into three dates, with each number preceded by an extraneous 1. This way,

the square becomes 1492—Columbus's discovery of North America; 1357—a son's and husband's ages; and 1816—when several volcanic eruptions produced "The Year Without Summer." Try devising other ways to remember these numbers in order.

$$4 \quad 9 \quad 2$$
$$3 \quad 5 \quad 7$$
$$8 \quad 1 \quad 6$$

3. This exercise shows an assortment of objects, most of which appear twice but some only once. Look through this collection for four minutes and then identify which objects are shown just once. Don't write down your answers as you go; instead, keep them in your working memory until you have finished, then write them down to check your answers.

Answer: The objects shown only once are the chicken, bicycle, sailboat, shoe, and house. Recognizing and remembering single items, particularly while you are deliberately not remembering items that appear twice, flexes your working memory.

4. While ordinary memory stores individual items in scratch-pad memory, Intelligent Memory enables you to form chunks of items in scratch-pad memory, thus broadening its capacity. Intelligent Memory does this by helping you find meaningful connections between items so that they stick with you. Such chunking is useful when it comes to important clumps of information, like numbers or dates that we have to remember. If you can't remember such facts in your life, use these examples as motivation to begin chunking your important information.

PIN number: Convert it into a month and a day that's a notable birthday.

Computer password: A friend uses the names of childhood pets and imagines each one at her feet when logging on.

Social Security number: The three groups of numbers can be remembered as a time and day, an amount of money, a series of weights or measurements, or as the ages of four people. Another possibility is to chunk the number according to an internal pattern—that is, numbers following a sequence, adding up to each other, or as mirror images of others.

A complicated procedure: Your cat needs regular shots and occasionally you must give the shot yourself. The vet gave you these instructions: Form an indent with the skin at the back of the cat's neck and stick the needle in, keeping it parallel to the cat's back. You might remember this procedure by thinking of "Make a tent—go through the opening."

Combination lock: A combination can be turned into a rhyme—for instance, 8R, 22L, 3R becomes, "Eight is two, two late to be free."

5. Here's a grid of 36 boxes, each containing a pattern. Some patterns appear in more than one box. Look through each row and mark the first time each pattern appears. As you look at each box, you must decide whether you've seen the pattern before or not (try not to look back). Take one minute to look through the entire grid and see if you can correctly mark the first appearance of each pattern.

Answer: This task stretches your scratch-pad memory more than other exercises because each line contains nine patterns, two more than the normal memory holds. Furthermore, some lines contain patterns that don't appear in other lines. It's hard to chunk these visually, but verbal labels might help you. You might find it easier if you give the patterns names: flag, M. C. Escher pattern, checkerboard, balls, dots.

6. This exercise is intended to test your auditory working memory—how well you hold things that you've heard. You use this memory constantly, especially in conversation. The best way to do this exercise is to have someone read you each list from left to right, and at the end of each line, ask you to repeat as many of the words as possible. If you can't find someone, however, read each list of words across, spending only a moment on each word, then cover it up and check your recall.

List 1:   mumps   school   switch   zinc   stoat   Greece   crew
          scroll   Maine   pen

List 2:   university   Louisiana   television   aluminum   biology
          dictionary   hippopotamus   uranium   academy   Australia

Answer: You probably noticed that you had an easier time remembering the first list, the monosyllabic words, than the second list, the polysyllabic words. (It also took you or your friend longer to read the second list.) Count yourself average if you recalled five or more of the monosyllabic words or three or more of the polysyllabic words. Given the short time between reading each list and trying to recall it, most of your recall came from your working memory, not from permanent memory. The monosyllabic words are a more direct test of your working memory, and help show you that its capacity is about five to nine items.

CHAPTER 6

Storing More Memories

What hasn't been saved can't be remembered. This makes storage the sine qua non of a fast, extensive Intelligent Memory, as well as of a good ordinary memory. For ordinary memory, remembering isolated facts is good enough. Intelligent Memory is more complicated because it requires that everything be stored in an organized way. Our Intelligent Memory depends not just on the quantity of information we've stored, but also on how that information is arranged in our memory. A well-organized Intelligent Memory lets us jump through connections. A disorganized memory is a barrier to our thoughts, sending them to wander aimlessly and come to dead ends.

The keys to making sure memories get organized as they are stored are threefold. First, you have to have the right organization or filing system. Second, you have to acquire memories or learn in a way that makes the best and most numerous connections between new and old memories.

Third, you have to pace your learning to allow connections between memories to become firmly cemented in your mind. When connections first form, they're fragile. Cramming in too much at once can overwrite them. By pacing the way you learn, you make your learning most efficient and most productive for your Intelligent Memory.

LIMITLESS SPACE

We can remember a large number of facts—not as many as a computer, nor as crisply or cleanly, but a large number nevertheless. In one test of the capacity of memory, students were shown 2,560 slides of individual faces. Each face was on the screen for only ten seconds. The whole viewing lasted a total of about seven hours, spread out over several days. An hour after the last slide was shown, the students were tested on another set of 2,560 slides. Each slide had a pair of faces on it, one which was a face that had been shown before. The students were asked to pick which of the two faces they had seen before. Despite the enormity of the task, most students were 85 to 95 percent accurate.

Memory also persists far longer than we might imagine. Fifty years after taking high school Spanish, adults who took the class still remembered some Spanish words and could read a little of it. Even if you thought you memorized history dates or French vocabulary just long enough to pass a test, some memory stays with you.

You've acquired many other kinds of memories much less deliberately. You've absorbed norms of social behavior and even filed away what you've read in newspapers. This information becomes a part of your permanent memory in much the same way that facts you deliberately committed to memory become a part of it. Learning "accidentally" this way is not as efficient as directly focusing your attention, as we've seen. But, through repeated exposures, your mind gradually soaks up almost everything you expose it to. This lifetime of information absorption is part of what gives your memory, and your Intelligent Memory, its power.

What makes Intelligent Memory even more vast and powerful than any computer memory is the way it's organized. Intelligent memories are not kept in isolated bins; they have multiple ties to each other so they can be queried in multiple ways. For example, try to answer these questions: What country is Paris in? Do you know the meaning of the word "mall"? What utensil do you use to cut food? How often does the

United States hold presidential elections? What do you do when you first meet someone? What's wrong with the sentence, "The threw boy ball the."? What's the main component of air? Do sharks have legs? Some answers you may know directly, from your memory. (That Paris is in France is likely to be one of these.) But you probably were never specifically taught that sharks don't have legs, so it's not a fact you had in memory. However, you probably could answer that sharks don't have legs as quickly, if not more quickly, than you could say that Paris was in France. No computer could do this as easily as you can. The reason lies in your Intelligent Memory and how it's organized. The word "sharks" is connected to a picture of sharks in your mind that does not include legs. Or, the word "sharks" may be connected to "fish," and you already know that fish have no legs. Either way, you probably answered no to the question faster than your conscious mind became aware of the reasoning you used. That was Intelligent Memory working.

You can answer countless questions like these quickly. Consider all you know about language, social customs, world affairs, geography, and humans and animals, not to mention all of your personal knowledge, like the breed of your dog or your employer's procedures for reimbursing expenses. All this information represents your nearly limitless capacity to store memories. Just as important, it demonstrates that these memories have been stored so they can be found and used flexibly.

Flexibility is the key. It allows you to look at what you have in your mind from perspectives totally different from the one you were using when you originally saved the information. How are sharks and trees alike? (They're both living, for one thing.) Flexibility allows you to use approximations to search your memory: Who do you know who acts like a shark? What breeds of dogs are similar to pugs?

To make this work, what you store in your memory needs to be stored in the right place. The right place means a niche in your mind where the information fits easily, can be extracted with little effort, and is clearly connected to other information. It's like storing a memo in a filing cabinet. The memo is important, so you want to keep it for a long time. You study the labels on the cabinet and consider how to file the document: By the name of the sender? By the date it was written? By topic? By subject reference line? You know that the label you choose will determine whether you'll be able to find it next year. If you must be absolutely sure that you can find it no matter what, you'll make copies of the memo and put it in every conceivable location. That's what your Intelligent Memory does too, in a way, except more efficiently. Intelligent Memory puts the name on the memo in one place, the date in another, the topic in yet another, and links them all together. Even though it looks like one memo to your mind, it's actually been cut into pieces and held together by connections.

FAMILIAR COMPANY

Pushing your memory is easier if you can connect with memories and categories you already have rather than create new ones from scratch. Each category is like a distinctive storage bin. Some have unique shapes, and some have bins within bins. Your uniquely shaped bins are your personal areas of expertise. If you're a photographer, you probably have a category for "camera lenses." If you're a cat fancier, you have a category for "feline diseases." Thus, it's easier to remember something similar to these other items in your memory than something unlike anything else you know. With no relevant information or existing context to attach new information to—no bin in place—the mind struggles to understand it and details can be forgotten or misconstrued. As an example, read the next paragraph and think about what it refers to:

> The procedure is actually quite simple. First, you arrange things into different groups depending on their makeup. Of course, one pile may be sufficient depending on how much there is to do. If you have to go somewhere else due to the lack of facilities, that is the next step; otherwise, you are pretty well set. It is important not to overdo any particular endeavor. That is, it is better to do too few things at once than too many. In the short run, this may not seem important, but complications from doing too many can easily arise. A mis-

take can be expensive as well. The manipulation of the appropriate mechanisms should be self-explanatory, and we need
not dwell on it here. At first, the whole procedure will seem
complicated. Soon, however, it will become just another facet
of life. It is difficult to foresee any end to the necessity for this
task in the immediate future, but one never can tell.

This paragraph contains instructions. What do you remember about
them? Without a category or context to give them meaning, probably
very little. All you've got in your mind is a collection of vague directions.
But reconsider the paragraph if you title it "Washing Clothes." Now it
makes sense. Instructions that were a hopeless jumble now become
meaningful. The category "washing clothes" allows you to give each instruction a context and connect them to a process you know.

Of course, remembering something completely new requires more
time and mental energy than remembering the familiar. Here are some
examples of how you can use this strategy to store information:

- You're studying accounting and learning the basics of book-
  keeping, including the rule that debits are always entered in the
  left column and credits are entered in the right column. It's
  likely, since you're just starting out, that the mental storage bin
  you already have for accounting is rather small. But if you're a
  driver, you have a large mental category related to driving on
  the right-hand side of the road. So you remember this accounting information as: right-side entry for money coming in, or
  credits (a good thing, like driving on the right side), and the left
  side for money going out, or debits (a bad thing, like driving on
  the left side). Eventually, with enough experience, the accounting bins will take on a life of their own, and support other connections themselves.
- You're going camping for the first time and have been told
  which snakes are poisonous and which are not. Snakes with
  black and red stripes are harmless, but those with yellow and
  red stripes are poisonous. While your storage bin for snake in-

formation is rather limited, your color category bin is huge. So you can best remember the facts you need to know about snakes by connecting them with the categories you already have for colors. Yellow in a traffic signal is a warning sign, and that's what you can connect it with to remember that yellow bands on a snake mean "caution."

ELABORATION

Elaboration saves information in many more places in your mind and makes it much easier to find when you search for it again. The best way to elaborate depends upon the material, and you. Linking to a familiar memory, visualizing, and giving the information more meaning are all variations on elaboration. If you can put the information into a coherent story, all the better. Most of us have great memories for stories. Many people unconsciously tell themselves stories. The hurricane season in the Caribbean is easy to remember with the help of this elaboration: "June too soon, July stand by, August a must, September remember, October all over." This is a wonderful elaboration because it not only rhymes but suggests a small story.

Large amounts of complicated information can be stored this way. One of the more extreme examples of this is when actors learn a script. Actors are expected to remember hours of dialogue flawlessly while acting at the same time. At auditions, they're expected to read scripts quickly and then perform them verbatim. These abilities astound the rest of us, but anyone can learn them. Actors use elaboration. As they read a script, they think of why each word was said the way it was: What is the intention behind the word? What is the effect of the word in the minds of the other characters? One study asked actors to read, from a script, a conversation between a man and a woman about love and possible infidelity.

Here's how one actor elaborated on just two words the female character asks as a question ("Well then . . . ?"), and the response he's to make according to the script (italics denote words in the script):

And she says, *"Well then . . . ?"*

Now she's asking me to explore the issue further by saying *"Well then . . . ?"*

And now I might as well tell her what I'm thinking that's bothering me: *"She wore it when I left with her."* Well, if she wore it when I left with her and it's here now and she's not here yet, then obviously she came back to see him. Or she came back for some reason and if I'm insecure about my fiancée's love, well, I could easily think that she came back to see [him].

Actors don't try to memorize specific words per se, but by concentrating on the larger meaning of the words, they remember them nevertheless. This same study examined how a famous professional mnemonist, Harry Lorayne, did on the same script. His memory was astounding compared to normal expectations, but he still remembered less of the script than the professional actors. His strategy was very different. As the authors of the study put it, "Lorayne appeared to look at the script from the outside, as information to be remembered; the actors appeared to look at it from the inside, as a life to be lived."

Even people with extraordinary memories, like the famed Russian mnemonist Shereshevskii, used stories to remember. He remembered the following formula by spinning a story.

$$N \cdot \sqrt{d^2 \times \frac{85}{vx}} \cdot \sqrt[3]{\frac{276^2 \cdot 86\,x}{n^2 v \cdot \pi\,264}} \quad n^2 b = sv\,\frac{1624}{32^2} \cdot r^2 s$$

Here's a sample from his story (the parentheses refer to elements of the formula): "Neiman (N) came out and poked with his stick ($\cdot$). He looked at a dried-up tree, which reminded him of a root (square-root symbol), and he thought: 'It is no wonder that this tree withered and that its roots were lain bare, seeing that it was already standing when I built these houses, these two here (d^2).' . . . He said, 'The houses are old, a cross ($\times$) should be placed on them.' This gives a great return on his original capital; he invested \$85,000 (85) in building them. The roof finishes off the building (—), and down below a man is standing and playing the harmonica (*vx*). . . ."

The story continues until Shereshevskii accounts for every symbol in the equation. Although few normal people would want to spin such an extensive story, if you think up a story that has personal meaning, you're much more likely to remember it.

Elaboration is easier the more you do it. Unlike other kinds of story spinning that you might share with friends or family, you can keep these to yourself and make them as outlandish as you like. A note of caution: Extremely bizarre elaborations may be so removed from your normal thinking that whatever help they provide in imprinting a memory may make it inaccessible later. For example, to remember that the capital of Arkansas is Little Rock, you might be tempted to imagine an animated ark sawing a little rock. Yet you may never again be in the state of mind where you'd think of an animated ark, let alone one that saws. And most rocks are broken, not sawed. If you make an elaboration reasonable, however, you strengthen meaningful connections without having to induce near-psychosis every time you want to remember something.

The more you elaborate, the better you store memories. When you direct more thought to the distinctive features of what you want to remember, you capture more of it. In an elaboration narrative, information can be woven together by chronology (like the hurricane rhyme), by cause and effect, by a connection to personal experiences, or by attaching it to existing knowledge or memories. Everyone's elaboration is different, each of us taps into unique thoughts or experiences. Here are other ways to elaborate:

- Use rhymes, which call on your vocabulary knowledge, to construct a meaningful memory. "Righty tighty, lefty loosy" is a great rhyme for remembering that handles and screws are turned to the right to make them tighter and to the left to loosen them. Even complex information can be stored this way, as long as the rhyme holds up.
- Songs or jingles, like rhymes, create patterns that make words easy to remember. Music combines words and phrases of man-

ageable lengths, adds distinctive emphasis, and engages help from your auditory memory. People given a list of words to remember while hearing background music readily recalled the words much later when they heard the same tune. To be useful, however, the melody has to be simple and easily repeated. One way to add music to something being remembered is to tap out a rhythm during the process.

- Elaborate on personal experiences to relate what you want to remember to what you already know. If you're an avid golfer and find yourself in a situation in which you want to remember how different-sized wrenches are used, you might relate each wrench to a particular golf club, like a wedge, three-iron, or driver.

- To remember complicated instructions that have more steps than your working memory can hold, visualize a diagram of what you are doing rather than try to remember the instructions in words. A visual diagram enables you to hold more information in your working memory.

- Devise a metaphor for information you're trying to capture, particularly if the information seems unrelated or from different areas, or if the material you're trying to remember is difficult.

ELABORATING FOR MEANING

Elaborating for meaning is a special sort of elaboration. It's a better way to elaborate because we're usually concerned with the meaning of what we're learning, not whether it rhymes with something. To see how well elaborating for meaning works, read these sentences, then cover them up and try to recall who did what.

1. The fat one bought the padlock.
2. The strong one cleaned the paintbrush.
3. The bald one cut out the coupon.
4. The poor one entered the museum.
5. The funny one admired the ring.

Now read elaborated versions of the sentences, then cover them up and recall who did what.

1. The fat one bought the padlock to attach to the refrigerator door.
2. The strong one cleaned the paintbrush in order to paint the barbells.
3. The bald one cut out the coupon for a free sample of Rogaine.
4. The poor one entered the museum to find shelter from the rain.
5. The funny one admired the ring that squirted water.

The second group of sentences is longer, but it also has more meaning than the first and should have made your memory storage easier.

REDUNDANT LOCATIONS

The more places you store information in your mind, the more likely it is that the information will persist and can be found. The particular form your mind uses to store information is called a code. Codes can be visual, auditory (as in rhymes), meaningful, or in other forms. Fortunately, multiple coding is almost automatic because of Intelligent Memory: You can't stop your mind from visualizing something when you see the word "elephant," and you can't stop your mind from saving that memory in at least two places—for the word itself and for the image of an elephant.

To exploit the benefits of multiple coding, you may have to devote some effort to finding different codes and connections. People differ in what codes and connections are easiest for them to remember, at least at the beginning. Most try to picture whatever it is they're trying to learn, finding this way to be relatively easy and powerful. Other people find they have a good memory for smells or tastes. They'll remember a trip to Italy not by visualizing Michelangelo's mural of the Last Supper, but by remembering the damp smell in the street after a rain. Yet other people remember sounds better, and for those, it may be helpful to code by sound: "Origami" would be remembered as rhyming with "salami." Whatever your particular set of associations, you make it harder to forget if you weave the new information into them. And perhaps most important, you make it part of an Intelligent Memory network that will persist long after the isolated fact you were trying to remember is forgotten.

As you encounter things and ideas you want to remember, consider them from as many perspectives as you can conjure up. Imagine you're examining a gem and want to study how the light hits each facet, so you slowly rotate it and view it from all angles. You'll find that each perspective offers a new image and so new places for storage. In essence, you're expanding the visual image of an idea so that it has more places in your mind to lodge.

VISUALIZING AND MNEMONICS

Coding in visual images is particularly useful for most of us because vision is one of our strongest memory systems. About 40 percent of the brain is devoted to vision functions—more than any other function. That's why your recognition memory for pictures—your ability to know if you've seen something before—is better than your memory for words or concepts. So if you can find a way to make something visual, it is bound to be remembered better.

You can save some words as visual images, depending on how concrete they are. The word "scissors" can be visualized easily, while "freedom" is abstract and more difficult to see. Visual storage happens automatically with concrete words because of the automatic connections in Intelligent Memory.

Mnemonics are sometimes dismissed as mental shortcuts that produce only game-show memory. It's true they're of only limited use to Intelligent Memory. Learning how to use them, however, is a good exercise in memory storage involving interactive imagery. Regardless of what's being remembered or for how long, storage is much easier with a well-oiled ability to use imagery.

Mnemonics have been around for ages—the Greeks are credited with coming up with the method called "loci," which uses location to fix something in memory and so is referred to as the "mental walk" method. It involves first conjuring a visual memory of a familiar place, such as your home, office, or backyard. It should be a place you know well and can recall in detail. You then imagine each individual thing you want to remember, and mentally place it in different locations within the familiar place. As you review what you want to remember— say, to buy gloves and a case of bottled water—you imagine each item at a specific place in the location or interacting with it, like seeing a pair of gloves on a garden chair and pouring a bottle of water into a bird-bath. When you want to recall your list of items or things to do, you take a mental walk around your familiar place, which will unpack your memory. This was the method used by nine of ten exceptional mne-monists in one study.

Another mnemonic, the peg method, pairs the numbers one to ten with an imagined object. The usual pairings are: One is a bun. Two is a shoe. Three is a tree. Four is a door. Five is a hive. Six is sticks. Seven is heaven. Eight is a gate. Nine is wine. Ten is a hen. Obviously, the num-bers and words rhyme, making them easier to remember. Once you've got these pairings down—and use vivid images for each, such as a foot-long hot dog bun—you imagine objects in relation to each other in-stead of remembering a sequence of numbers. If you want to remember three things you have to do in the morning—say, pay the electricity bill, water the flowers, and buy panty hose—you create these images: your electric bill rolled up, covered with mustard inside a bun, a shoe stepping on your flowers, a pair of panty hose hanging from a tree.

The peg system helps in many kinds of situations. We have a friend who credits it with helping in his career, especially when he's selling. He's the CEO of a successful publicly held company and learned the peg method when he was in the air force training to be a combat pilot. On bombing missions he needed to remember instrument numbers and lots of other information in order to make split-second decisions. He says that the peg system has now helped him become a effective salesman—he never forgets names, numbers, or lists of things to do.

Memory contest champions often rely on techniques like exaggerat-ing people's facial features to generate a cue and name they can remem-ber. Another technique is coding pairs of numbers to remember vast strings of digits. A pair of numbers is given a meaningful code, for example, 00 = bicycle, as in two wheels; 57 = tomato sauce, as in Heinz varieties; and 39 = Hitler, as in the year he started World War II. With this system, the number 395700 would be visualized as Hitler grabbing a bottle of ketchup, then riding a bike. Using this system, one memory expert was able to remember 15,000 phone numbers in Blackpool, England.

No matter what the specific method, all mnemonics are based on the same principles: linking what needs to be learned with what is already known; storing in multiple locations; putting additional attention and interest into the act of learning, so that it is deeper and more permanent; and storing with cues that make it easy to find the information again. And of course, using mnemonics is also another way of repeating what you want to remember to yourself.

As far as Intelligent Memory is concerned, all of these mnemonics are inferior to remembering by meaning or substance. They let you remember information, but they don't add to it's value. However, if you have to remember something, they do work. Even professional actors use mnemonics to master particularly tricky combinations of words or lyrics. Mel Brooks and Anne Bancroft both used mnemonic tricks to learn how to sing lyrics in Polish for their movie *To Be or Not to Be.*

REPEATING AND REHEARSING

The way you repeat and practice what you're trying to remember influences how readily you store it. "Talking through" what you're learning—adding explanations to yourself—and understanding the concepts makes the information more usable later. Repeating and applying thoughtful practice, as opposed to rote memorization, creates new neurological connections in the brain. Scans of an expert and novice doing the same activity show different areas of activity in the brain and indicate that the expert's thoughts involve more complexity. In practical terms, this means that the expert is learning more quickly, will remember more, and will be able to apply what he's remembered to a wider variety of situations.

A common form of rehearsal among experts is mental practice. A concert musician thinks through how she will play every passage in a piece before stepping on the stage. An experienced runner thinks about every hill, flat stretch, and turn in an upcoming race. The repetition seems easy enough, but we often have to be reminded to do it. It's easy to get careless and perhaps repeat something in our head once or twice, then let it go. The most effective repetition goes beyond a couple of run-throughs and, more important, is done aloud. Our auditory memory, even when it's our own voice, is especially powerful when we don't have a visual image to help boost memory.

Repetition alone is a weak way of learning. It's far more effective to rehearse with elaboration, of any kind. Have you ever heard a joke, admonished yourself to remember it, then promptly forgot it? If you had rehearsed the actual telling of the joke, with all its gestures and expressions, you probably would have remembered it better. Rehearsing is a form of elaboration, for each time you think through the material, you're expanding on it.

Rehearsing is especially important when you're trying to remember a process, such as how to change a tire. The memory of the steps will be even more lasting if, as you're practicing them, you understand the logic or underlying reasons for them. It's always easier to remember events that follow some kind of order as opposed to a collection of random occurrences. If you understand the reason for the order, in your own mind you'll be creating a minimind out of a set of rules that can eventually perform the task with hardly a thought. You've learned not just knowledge but how to use it.

SPACED PRACTICE

How would you like to remember better while spending less time trying to learn? Wishful thinking? It's actually been done for years. The trick is not to try to learn something all at once. Instead, learn in small increments spread over a longer period of time. You will spend less total amount of time learning, and what you learn will be stored more accurately and more thoroughly.

This has been proven repeatedly. A few years ago, British letter carriers were given a course in how to type so they could use new postal codes when sorting the mail. The postal employees could enroll in one of four classes of varying degrees of intensity and concentration. One class was the most intense, with two two-hour sessions each day. Another class was the most leisurely, with one one-hour session a day but not every day. The group with the most intensive schedule—four hours a day—needed 80 hours of instruction to learn to type an acceptable number of correct keystrokes a minute. The group that worked only one hour a day learned to type as well after only 50 hours of instruction. Even months after the course ended, the one-hour-a-day group retained their skills better than the four-hours-a-day group. The one drawback to spreading out practice or memory sessions is that the process itself lasts for a longer period of time.

This is not an isolated example. The principle is so well known that it's been given a name: the spacing effect. Spacing works for several reasons. One is that it's easier to concentrate for short, intense periods of time. While it may appear that two hours of class must be better than one, the amount of time in which anybody can learn effectively in a single sitting is often less than an hour, so the extra time is wasted. In an hour, attention doesn't wander as much and external thoughts can be less distracting because you know you will finish soon.

Spaced-out learning also works because the new memories have less chance to interfere with old learning. Interference is a major cause of forgetting. By separating episodes of learning, you allow each instance of learning to become more distinct in your mind. Also, spacing gives your brain time to replenish nutrients and chemicals that build memories that are depleted during learning. The additional time lets new connections gain strength.

Finally, spacing allows what we are learning to percolate more widely in our minds and make broader contact with other memories. It's akin to the difference between a steady, light rainfall that gets a chance to soak into the ground and a heavy downpour that runs off before it has a chance to soak in. The intermittent steady rain is like spaced remembering and the downpour is like cramming your memory. This slower yet deeper learning makes spaced learning better for fostering Intelligent Memory.

YOUR BRAIN'S SECOND SHIFT

Storing memories from scratch-pad memory into long-term memory doesn't occur only while we're awake. There's a growing body of research suggesting that your brain can make this transfer while you're asleep. There may be even a greater amount of permanent learning occurring during sleep than wakefulness. It's still being debated, as are other questions about the type of material best learned during sleep (skills or facts, for example) and what part of sleep does the trick (dreaming or non-dreaming sleep). Nevertheless, your memory doesn't gel as well when you haven't had enough sleep. Your mother was right about the value of a good night's sleep.

EXERCISES

1. To see how a little extra thought improves your memory storage, try this exercise.

- Answer each question for the word that follows it:

Is this word in lower case?	dog
Is this word in upper case?	apple
Is this word in lower case?	SOLDIER
Is this word in upper case?	TELEPHONE
Is this word in lower case?	raincoat
Is this word in upper case?	TUMBLE
Is this word in lower case?	jogging
Is this word in upper case?	redhead
Is this word in lower case?	savvy
Is this word in upper case?	CINEMA

- Now cover the list and try to recall as many of the words as possible. Make a note of how many you remembered.
- Next, read and answer these questions.

Does this word rhyme with hand?	interrupt
Is this the name of a vegetable?	California
Is this word in upper case?	misty
Is this the name of an animal?	skunk
Does this word rhyme with Sunday?	monthly
Is this word in upper case?	MEOW
Is this the make of a car?	Toyota
Does this word rhyme with shoe?	blue
Is this word in upper case?	price
Is this a kind of food?	lotion

- Again cover the list and recall as many words as possible.

Explanation: Your recall on the second list should be much better than that on the first because the questions in the second required more thinking. You had to consider not only how the word was written (upper or lower case), but also its meaning or sound. This is a simple version of what you do when you store memories—form images, ask questions, consider perspectives—because that's how things get solidified into many places in your permanent memory.

2. Following are two sets of questions. Answer the first group and note how long it takes you, then do the same with the second.

GROUP 1

Name a fruit beginning with the letter S.   _____

Name an animal beginning with the letter P.   _____

Name a bird beginning with the letter R.   _____

Name a country beginning with the letter T.   _____

Name a famous actor beginning with the letter C.   _____

Name a famous actress beginning with the letter B.   _____

Name a vegetable beginning with the letter A.   _____

Name a flower beginning with the letter D.   _____

GROUP 2

Name a fruit ending with the letter A.   _____

Name an animal ending with the letter G.   _____

Name a bird ending with the letter D.   _____

Name a country ending with the letter O.   _____

Name a famous actor ending with the letter Y.   _____

Name a famous actress ending with the letter P.   _____

Name a vegetable ending with the letter S.   _____

Name a flower ending with the letter T.   _____

> *Explanation:* Odds are good that you quickly answered the questions in Group 1 but were much slower finishing Group 2. The reason lies in the way you store information. How we store determines how easily or how hard it is to retrieve. We store names by their first letter, not by the third or last letter. We store them according to categories, which makes it easier to narrow our search. We have no last-letter category, so we're left to randomly scroll through the names we know, testing each to see if the last letter matches what we're looking for. This is why the names of items beginning with a particular letter quickly came to mind, while you had to search through an entire category, trying out each one, in order to find a last-letter match.

3. Finding a category can add meaning to information and make it easier to remember. To show you the difference:

- Read each sentence, taking no more than five seconds for each.

    Steve walked on the roof.
    Harry picked up the egg.

Bill hid the axe.
Jim flew the kite.
Frank flipped the switch.
Al built a boat.
Sam hit his head on the ceiling.
Adam quit his job.
Jack fixed the sail.
Ed wrote the play.

- To test your memory, cover up the sentences and answer these questions:

Who built the boat?
Who picked up the egg?
Who walked on the roof?
Who quit his job?
Who flew the kite?
Who fixed the sail?
Who hit his head on the ceiling?
Who wrote the play?
Who flipped the switch?
Who hid the axe?

- Chances are your mind had no ready category for the statements. Without being able to store them alongside familiar memories, you were hard pressed to hold on to them. Now read the next ten questions, again spending only five seconds on each.

Steve and Santa Claus walked on the roof.
Harry and the Easter bunny picked up the egg.
Bill and George Washington hid the axe.
Jim and Benjamin Franklin flew the kite.
Frank and Thomas Edison flipped the switch.
Al and Noah built a boat.
Sam and Michael Jordan hit their heads on the ceiling.

Adam and Richard Nixon quit his job.
Jack and Christopher Columbus fixed the sail.
Ed and William Shakespeare wrote the play.

- Again cover the statements and answer these questions:

Who built the boat?
Who picked up the egg?
Who walked on the roof?
Who quit his job?
Who flew the kite?
Who fixed the sail?
Who hit his head on the ceiling?
Who wrote the play?
Who flipped the switch?
Who hid the axe?

Now you've got categories to work with and preexisting knowledge to hook up with. This makes the information you're trying to learn much easier to understand, to store, and to recall, even though you actually had to remember a bit more with the second set of sentences. Using this method of finding familiar company may take some time, especially for material that is really new. But it builds on the memories you already have.

Thoughtful storing of memories and knowledge builds a strong foundation for Intelligent Memory. So far in this process, you have been laying groundwork, assembling the pieces, and thoughtfully arranging them so that putting them together to form Intelligent Memory will be as easy as painting by numbers. The next step in the process, expanding connections, is what ignites Intelligent Memory. In the next chapter we show you how to link memories into powerful chains.

CHAPTER 7

Sparking Connections

Connections are what make Intelligent Memory intelligent. Connections allow one thought to link with another to create chains of ideas that solve a problem or lead to a new thought. Each new connection adds more to Intelligent Memory than just a single idea or piece of information. It opens up hundreds or thousands of new routes in your mind.

Connections are formed in several ways. They develop as the natural by-product of all your learning, because the learning itself involves automatically generating associations. Reach for an apple and a computer company might spring to mind. Conscious, imaginative thinking does this even more. Imagine yourself biting into an apple, and the sight, taste, juiciness, and crunch of an apple all get fused a little more strongly in your mind. You can also force your mind to make connections by juxtaposing images, ideas, and thoughts in general.

DO YOU MAKE CONNECTIONS?

Jokes are a good way of exposing the connections you have and illustrating how you make new ones. Until the punch line, your existing connections lead you down a predictable path of assumptions, concepts, and meanings. But at the last minute, the joke jumps off its path to an entirely different one, and you've created a new connection. This is what happens when you "get" a joke: There's a collision between the expected and unexpected, and we laugh when we realize we've been tricked. This collision exposes the connections used for Intelligent Memory. See if you can identify the streams of thought or meanings that collide in these jokes.

- Microsoft's Bill Gates is talking with the chairman of General Motors, bragging about the advances of his industry. He says, "If automotive technology had kept pace with computer technology over the past few decades, you'd now be driving a V-32 instead of a V-8 and it would have a top speed of ten thousand miles an hour."

  "Sure," says the chairman, "but I really wouldn't want to drive a car that crashes four times a day."

- Two gentlemen, both hard of hearing and strangers, were about to ride the London Underground. One of them, studying the station they were entering, said, "Pardon me, but is this Wembley?"

  "No," said the other man, "Thursday."

  "No," said the first man, "I've already had a drink."

- Did you hear about the Italian chef who died? He pasta way.

- Jones was having difficulty with the telephone. "Ottiwell," he was saying. "I want to speak to Reginald Ottiwell."

  The operator said, predictably, "Would you spell the last name?"

  Jones began, "O as in Oscar, T as in Thomas, T as in Thomas again, I as in Irene, W as in Wallace . . ."

  At which point the operator interrupted, "W as in what?"

"No, no,—not a pride! It's a bunch of tourists."

(2003, The New Yorker Collection from cartoonbank.com. All rights reserved.)

WHAT'S SO FUNNY?

The Bill Gates joke invites assumptions and meanings associated with computers, then jumps to another meaning for the word "crash." The hard-of-hearing strangers joke is a word play that uses sounds as a setup for a collision of meanings. The pasta joke is obviously a pun that amuses us because it uses "pasta" to suggest "passed" away

However, if you didn't laugh at the operator joke, you have lots of company. Many people hesitate before finding the humor here. For a joke to get an instant laugh, the collision between the expected and unexpected has to be immediate. Like the others, this joke depends on a collision, in this case one between sense and nonsense, but the nonsense isn't clear at first because the operator's question sounds reasonable. Only when you think about it—it doesn't matter what word is used to illustrate W as long as the operator knows it's a W—does the humor surface.

The final joke, the cartoon, flips the animal and human worlds, showing the lions having the same "intelligent" discussion that people have about the curious names applied to groups of things.

What makes a joke funny is the same kind of thinking that triggers Intelligent Memory. Both depend on connecting at least two distinctive concepts or trains of thought. To make a joke, you create new combinations—pairings of images or concepts that you haven't made before.

In everyday uses of Intelligent Memory, the connections don't have to be completely novel or whimsical; they just have to be useful. In either case, you'll discover a connection that you didn't know you had, stretch connections that you did have, or create entirely new ones.

BUILDING BETTER CONNECTIONS

All of our memories have connections. It's impossible to think of a solitary idea or concept or experience or fact. Every memory sparks connections. Most of these connections are common and predictable. Psychologists are famous for tapping into these common connections or associations to gauge how someone's thinking veers from the norm. A hundred years ago, Carl Jung devised a word association test that is still used today. You would probably recognize the word pairings or connections that he found to be "normal," such as head—foot, window—room, pay—bills, and table—chair. You can see where some less common associations, like the ones below, come from, but they're not the first or the strongest connections in most people's minds:

Window—icon
Head—honcho
Table—plateau
Fund—hedge

Yet another way of understanding the kinds of connections you normally make is by deliberately violating them. How do these statements strike you?

I ate a building for breakfast.
Joe shivered from the warm water.
The pencil can't see very well.
This book is very happy.

Of course, these connections could be commonplace in some situations. Godzilla probably does eat buildings for breakfast, and as for Joe shivering in the warm water—some people are cold no matter what. Both the pencil and the book could be cartoon characters. But interpreting these metaphorically requires you to make novel connections.

Our normal connections generally work well and allow us to link the most useful or germane thoughts. For example, when driving, we instantly link the brightened taillights of a car in front of us with the act of pressing the brakes. We link the feel of our car skidding with turning the steering wheel. When you learned to drive, you formed a connection between the idea of controlling direction and the steering wheel. Years of driving have cemented the connection, and it's now so established in your mind that you don't even think about it when your car starts sliding.

This normal connection doesn't work in every situation, however. For instance, when driving on ice, or when your car begins to slide into a skid, you must forge a new connection between skidding and turning the steering wheel in a different direction than your instinctive reaction. When a car skids, most people turn against the skid to straighten the wheels. On ice, or when sliding, your normal connection is not helpful, so you need to establish a new one.

It is the same with solving everyday problems. Most of the time, you use the well-established connections and routines in your Intelligent Memory to solve them: The family pet is sick, so you take it to the veterinarian. But if on the day the pet is sick, you don't have time to go to the vet, you need to do something different. Necessity forces you to discover that you can call a mobile vet to make a house call. In the future, your Intelligent Memory will have this as an option.

Since Intelligent Memory is used in almost everything we do, so are connections. The connections we're concerned with here happen in fractions of a second. Dozens if not hundreds of connections are active at the same moment in almost anything we do. If we're trying to stretch our minds, we may be working even longer chains that churn over hours or days.

There are a number of ways to get your mind to make connections. You might start with a single item and think about its properties or features. A man was combing the burrs out his dog's fur one day when he wondered what made them sticky. Velcro fasteners were the result. Or you might try pairing two items and finding points of similarity or difference. Sometimes this pairing has a practical purpose. In developing a new product, for example, you might want to combine the best features of two different products.

Such thinking has given us landing lights for toilet seats (for sitting in the dark), an alarm fork (beeps when you eat too fast), a pet toilet, a tricycle lawnmower (so the kids can use their energy to help cut the lawn), and a motorized ice cream cone (to push the ice cream into our mouths so we don't have to slurp it from the cone with our tongues). These all may sound bizarre, but all have received U.S. patents. And the Pet Rock actually made it onto many people's desks for a time.

STRETCH FOR NOVELTY

The connections that we're proudest of and the ones that help the most are completely novel. Some are novel in an amusing way and some are so novel as to seem completely fantastic. Unless something is already perfect, there is always the possibility of having a thought, developing a process, or coming up with an idea that is better.

Artists are known for coming up with utterly novel ideas. Sometimes such novelty takes just one additional connection. For example, everybody has wrapped something—a gift, a sore foot—in their lives. The artist Christo extended this idea. He's been celebrated for the past forty years for wrapping entire buildings, forests, and even canyons. His wrapping, novel in its scale, is considered by many to be an important artistic statement and a work of art. Similarly, everybody has tapped out a rhythm on a trash-can lid or some makeshift surface. *Stomp,* the Off-Broadway musical, makes this the music of an entire show. Not only trash cans but plastic buckets and iron pipes are used to make its rhythms.

Artists are not the only people trying to forge connections to make something new and useful. Businesspeople, parents, athletes—anyone grappling with a dilemma or looking for a better way—seek out new connections, too. Not all connections correspond to something in the real world; sometimes they involve pulling things apart that people just assumed belonged together. For example, a multibillion-dollar financial market was built up around derivatives, which resulted when someone realized that the risk associated with the interest paid on loans, which was considerable, could be separated from the risk of the principal of the loan itself, which was small. Adventurous investors were willing to gamble on the risks of the interest; more conservative investors would opt for the principal. Suddenly, two secondary markets were made out of one loan. This may seem esoteric, but chances are now high that any loan you have is being handled this way.

There are several things to keep in mind as you imagine sprouting connections to solve all your problems. They wouldn't be problems if they had easy solutions, so expect to have to try a great many new connections and follow a great many routes before you find something better than you currently have—if you ever do. If you push for numerous novel associations, you will also churn up noise and junk and weird pairings that have no useful value. But if you *don't* push, you are guaranteed to never find anything useful. It's like panning for gold—you have to sift through a lot of dirt to have a better chance of finding the nuggets.

People recognized as brilliant thinkers and inventors know this. Almost every one of them has a story of innumerable tries before hitting on the right combination. Thomas Edison obtained patents for 1,093 unique ideas, yet few were on a par with the electric lightbulb, phonograph, or moving pictures. Picasso created more than 20,000 works of art, but only a fraction of them are counted as masterpieces. What counts in these cases is that these "inventors" did produce masterpieces. But don't forget how much probing of connections and possibilities it took to make them.

FORMING A WEB WITH ANALOGIES

Analogies are one important way to make leaps from one element in memory to another. The analogies that generate Intelligent Memory may be as rudimentary as those between single words (*snow* is to *flake* as *rain* is to *drop*, for example), or as complex as metaphors, similes, and figures of speech (*"Get out of bed, you slug!"*). Or the analogy may be between one complex idea and another, or even between entire philosophical systems.

To understand how thinking in analogies can help solve a problem, read this anecdote about the James Bond movie *Goldfinger*. (You'll be asked to apply an analogy from it to a problem later in this chapter.)

> Auric Goldfinger is somehow smuggling large quantities of gold out of England. He travels constantly between England and Europe, moving in a luxurious custom-built car chauffeured by his menacing bodyguard, Oddjob. Each time Goldfinger leaves England, officials thoroughly search his car and all his other possessions, but have never been able to find where he hides the gold. Finally, Bond follows Goldfinger after he arrives in Europe and discovers him in a secret smelter. Bond has a flash of insight [what we now know to be a sudden connection in Intelligent Memory]—the gold was never in the car. The car itself is the gold. No one else had had this insight, so all their searches were fruitless.

Making an analogy requires loosening the boundaries or definitions of the parts that are to be matched. It focuses on general features or functions and ignores details that are irrelevant in that context. Nature is an easy, ready source for all sorts of analogies, such as visual or functional comparisons. Analogies inspired by nature frequently trigger unusual pairings and novel solutions.

A new design for the roof of a large industrial building found an analogy with a fish, the flounder, which changes color to match its surroundings by exposing or retracting tiny sacs of black pigment on its skin. The flounder's camouflage sparked the idea of using black and white on the building's roof to alter the interior's temperature. The design has an all-black roof that is studded with little white plastic balls. In warm weather, the plastic balls expand and show their white parts, which reflect sunlight and heat. In cold weather, the balls contract and the black surfaces soak up heat.

While there are numerous ways of conjuring up analogies, most of the methods begin with distilling your problem or situation into general features or bigger concepts. Scientists often think this way. When Ben Franklin was designing his experiment that used a kite to connect two phenomena—lightning and electricity—that no one had yet put together, he noted these similarities between them: light producing, crooked direction, swift motion, conducted by metals, a crack or noise in exploding. When the architect Frank Gehry was considering possible shapes for the buildings he was designing, he remembered images from his childhood of undulating silver fish.

The managers of a dating service, looking for better ways to match up their members, were inspired by the idea of fast-food service. Patrons of both want lots of choices, quick service, and an efficient, fuss-free operation. It may sound like a stretch—looking for love and buying a burger—but the connection produced SpeedDating, the latest phenomena among the in-search-of crowd. Like driving through McDonald's, a SpeedDating event involves a quick exchange—a series of seven-minute conversations between willing singles. Those who enjoy the first meeting can later go back to someone for seconds.

There are various ways of conjuring up an analogy. You can imagine yourself as part of the activity or situation. For instance, assume you're fixing something in the house and need to shine a light into a small space at the end of lots of twists and turns. Visualizing yourself as the light, weaving your way left and right, up and down, might give you the same idea that occurred to the toolmaker Black & Decker. Its SnakeLight is a thin flashlight attached to the end of a long, flexible tube that can fit into all sorts of nooks and crannies.

Another approach is to jump boundaries and look beyond the immediate problem to another arena. A potato chip company found a parallel between good packaging and bagging autumn leaves, which is best done if the leaves are wet. Wet leaves clump, making them easier to pick up and press together. As a result, the company designed a wet potato mixture that it molded into chips and packaged in a tube. This analogy produced the Pringles potato chip.

Human biology is also rich in potential analogies. Bicyclists needed a water bottle that would squirt water but not let mud seep in. The tricuspid valve of the human heart became the inspiration for the flaps used as the spout of a new bottle.

A third way of coming up with an analogy is to insert your thinking into a different part of the problem. This is how the inventor of the car-theft device, The Club, came up with the idea. Although Jim Winner's new Cadillac had an alarm system, the car was stolen soon after he bought it. In devising a way to prevent his next car from being stolen, he didn't dwell on making a better lock. Instead, he thought about ways to stop a thief from driving the car. He recalled his time in the army when he prevented fellow soldiers from using his Jeep by wrapping a thick metal chain around the steering wheel and attaching it to the brake. Envisioning a thief trying to make off in his car, he figured, "Can't steer, can't steal."

Wild imaginings are another route to finding an analogy solution. This involves little more than thinking up fantastic scenarios and isn't far from the amusingly impossible ideas that five-year-olds conjure. One of the most famous wild imaginings that solved a problem came from Albert Einstein. In trying to understand the relativity of time, Einstein imagined a person inside a streetcar that was speeding away from a large clock. He wondered what the clock would read if the streetcar were going at the speed of light, the same speed it took the image of the clock to travel to the eyes of the passenger. Since the passenger and the light reflecting off the clock were moving at the same speed, the image of the clock wouldn't change. It would appear as if time was standing still. Einstein realized that the measurement of time was dependent on speed.

Many people have difficulty finding similarities between problem-solving strategies, especially when two situations look completely different. The trick is to go beyond the specifics of an individual situation to try to find common operational principles. Try solving this problem:

A peasant who lived near the border of his country found work in a neighboring country and so traveled there every day. Each day as he was crossing the border, the guards thoroughly searched him and his wheelbarrow, looking for anything of value that they could tax. Some days he carried manure and on other days, straw or dirt. They were certain he was smuggling something because so many of the country's inhabitants were trying to escape its repressive government. Many months went by with their cat-and-mouse game, the guards always searching his wheelbarrow and the peasant always declaring nothing. The guards never found anything. Years later, one of the guards encountered the peasant in a tavern and asked for the true story. The peasant admitted that he had been smuggling. How did he do it?

If you saw the analogy with the Goldfinger scenario, you were right: The peasant was smuggling parts of the wheelbarrow.

Having seen this analogy, do you see the similarities between these two classic problems?

A patient has an inoperable tumor. It can be treated only by radiation, but large doses will harm the surrounding healthy tissue. How can the tumor be treated without destroying healthy tissue?

The dictator of a small country is under siege by a rebel army. The dictator has taken refuge in a fortress in the heart of the country's farmland. The fortress has enough supplies to last for months and the dictator's army has laid land mines under all the roads leading into the fortress. Any heavy activity on the roads leading to the fortress would trigger the mines. The rebels are too poor to have planes. How can the rebels successfully attack the fortress?

Although vastly different, both problems are analogous in their structure and solution. You probably noticed the similarities between the tumor and the fortress—each needs to be destroyed, yet the attack has to be limited because they are surrounded by areas that can sustain only minor damage. With similar problems come similar solutions.

What's needed in both examples is a convergence of forces. With the tumor, the answer is to direct numerous beams of low-level radiation from different angles to converge at the tumor. This is the actual method that is widely used today in radiation therapy. For the fortress, sending small bands of rebels on the roads leading into it allows them to pick around the mines, then coordinate the attack to assault the fortress walls at the same time.

Of course, don't let the definite similarity between two problems blind you to their unique aspects. Just recently, advances in surgical treatment have allowed surgical teams to take a cancerous liver completely out of a patient's body, radiate it to the maximum, and then replace it in the same person. That way, no surrounding tissue is damaged at all.

A LONG, LOOSE CHAIN

Many seemingly simple connections that pop to mind, like using a car key as a knife to rip open a tight plastic wrapping, involve more than a one-step association or a single analogy. In the case of the car key, the intermediate connective steps might have been from key to other tools that open, to tools that cut, pierce, or rip. In essence, the idea of using a car key to tear open a package involves a string of analogies.

Sometimes finding a new connection with a single analogy doesn't deliver the solution you're seeking. The comparison is not distinctive or special enough to address the situation. You may need to think further and loosen your thinking so that even more remote associations can surface. A chain of thoughts made of a series of small mental steps leading away from the starting idea can expand your connection network. The chain may consist of a series of analogies or vaguely related associations. Many people use this technique to jog their memories, probing for small hints or clues that will trigger a recollection. Middle-aged people trying to remember the names of high school classmates typically begin with details about the school, its facilities and locale, where classmates lived, and routes to their homes. If you're trying to remem-

ber what the weather was like last Monday, you might begin with recalling what you wore and what you did.

During World War II, a British engineer was playing with his son at
a duck pond and got the idea for a new kind of bomb. He had been
wrestling with the problem of how to destroy key dams in Germany's
Ruhr Valley. Existing bombs were so inaccurate that they were often
miles off target. Furthermore, the most vulnerable part of a dam is its
base. Although a torpedo would destroy them, the dams were in land-
locked waters and impossible for submarines to get to.

As the engineer and his son began skipping stones across the water, he
wondered if he could design a bomb that would bounce off the water as
it traveled and detonate only when it hit the dam directly. From a duck
pond, to skipping stones, to bouncing bombs, the engineer came up with
"Bouncing Betty," a bomb that some people say altered the course of the
war. The bouncing bomb smashed two German dams, creating a flood
that destroyed plants, factories, and bridges for a hundred miles.

GIANT STEPS WITH BRAINSTORMING

Coming up with the associations or ideas that can form a chain may
take some mental stretching. Many of us tend to be a little rigid in our
thinking; our imagination doesn't go wild very often. We don't easily
bounce between levels of analogies or make great mental leaps, min-
gling various kinds of knowledge or ideas. Brainstorming is a handy
way to make such giant steps.

Most people are familiar with brainstorming, thinking that it's what
they do when they toss around ideas. But it's more than that. While often used by groups of people, brainstorming can be used by individuals
on their own. The principles are the same, though a single person will
produce fewer ideas than a group. A few basic rules need to be followed
if it's to work well.

First, the main goal should be quantity. The more ideas the better, regardless of their content. Second, judgment has to be completely sus-
pended until the end of the process. Thoughts about ideas being stupid,

silly, impractical, or anything else that implies that they're unacceptable must be shelved. "Don't drive with your brakes on when trying to come up with ideas," advises the father of brainstorming, Alex Osborn. Third, try to piggyback ideas, using one as a springboard or as the centerpiece of a combination of ideas. Fourth, ignore logic and the need to make sense. Ideas that are nonsense or impossible can spark others. A benefit of individual brainstorming is that you may feel less inhibited in thinking up wacky ideas. Fifth, all ideas should be written down because you're going to be producing many of them. You don't want to forget them; when you're evaluating, you may find connections that you didn't see before.

The designers at the product design firm Ideo, which came up with the ideas for the Apple mouse and PalmPilot, regularly use brainstorming to spur thinking and generate enthusiasm. In a session to think up new designs for a shopping cart, they produced off-the-wall ideas: Velcro kid seats with matching diapers so that toddlers would "stick" inside the cart; a privacy shade for someone buying condoms by the case. Many food stores now offer "miniature" shopping carts that have baskets at two levels and a side rack for purchases that can be hung, like a six-pack of drinks connected by plastic webbing. These could well have been the product of brainstorming.

Don't let brainstorming put you off because it feels chaotic. That's the way it's supposed to feel. People typically halt their brainstorming because it seems unproductive, but the best ideas surface not at the beginning but after you've been doing it for a while. So, when you're tempted to quit, give yourself another five minutes and see what pops up.

INCUBATING FOR CREATIVE CONNECTIONS

Sometimes even the most creative, far-flung thinking doesn't produce a great connection. When this happens, it's time to turn away and think about anything *but* the problem. If you can let a problem stew for a few hours or a day, incubation may provide the answer. Although it's difficult to ignore a problem that's nagging you, quiet gestation has a great track record for producing breakthrough solutions.

Neuroscientists don't understand exactly why incubation works, although they have theories. A theory that makes sense ascribes the success of incubation to deliberately forgetting or ignoring the ideas in working memory that you've been pushing around and that haven't produced a worthwhile solution. By doing this, your mind turns away from unproductive connections, dead ends, and wrong guesses, and your unconscious gets fresh material to work with—buried memories and associations. It's important to emphasize that incubating is about *not* consciously thinking or remembering, and about deliberately ignoring immediate ideas so that buried thoughts mingle and germinate.

Letting your mind churn away while you sleep often works. This is how the nineteenth-century chemist Friedrich Kekule produced a novel theory of the molecular structure of benzene. While he was napping, Kekule dreamed of a cavorting snake that circled on itself to bite its tail. This circular structure was exactly what he was looking for.

Of course, you don't have to be asleep for your ideas to percolate. Johannes Brahms, the composer, said that his best musical ideas came to him while shining his shoes. Joseph Conrad soaked in the bathtub when he needed to think up new ideas. William Hewlett, one of the founders of the Hewlett-Packard Corporation, noted, "Actually, you probably do most of your thinking not at work. I do it when I'm trying to get to sleep at night, in the shower in the morning, or shaving. I suppose this says that you're really thinking about the job most of the time. There are so many day-to-day distractions that I consider important that it's really hard to sit down and do any concentrated thinking."

Engaging in a distraction that demands concentration provides a fertile opportunity for idea incubation. A popular sport among physicists is technical mountain climbing—scaling slick or icy walls hundreds of feet high. Technology companies frequently create opportunities for their employees to chew on problems. A Boston company built its employees a miniature golf course in its headquarters and moved a Ping-Pong table into its lunchroom.

Whether you engage in a sport or visit a museum, it's all fodder for incubation. By exposing yourself to new materials, new associations, and new places, you're tucking away the raw materials of new connections.

EXERCISES

1. Look at each inkblot and come up with two ordinary ideas and two unusual ideas for what they resemble.

Figure 1

Figure 2

Figure 3

Explanation: These blotches are similar to those of the famed Rorschach test. Here are some of the ideas we produced for this exercise, to compare with your own: For Figure 1, the ordinary ideas were smudges and dark clouds. The unusual ideas were magnetized iron filings and a man in a hat hurrying along on a dark windy day, trying to get home before it rains. For Figure 2, the ordinary ideas were an ape and a boxer. The unusual ideas were an ice hockey player holding another player's jersey and Rodin's *The Thinker* shouting "Eureka!" Figure 3 inspired the ordinary ideas of an African voodoo dancer and a cactus plant. The extraordinary ideas it triggered were a Mexican in a sombrero running up a long hill to escape rain clouds and a boy careening down a hill on a skateboard.

2. Can you identify the different ideas being linked in the following word combinations?

A. Financial watchdog
B. Bureaucratic bottleneck
C. Food chain
D. Internet superhighway
E. Moral bankruptcy

Answers:

A. Money and the act of guarding.
B. The gridlock of a large organization and the narrow exit point from a bottle.
C. The steps in growing or marketing and the links of a chain.
D. The fast, electronic connections in the World Wide Web and a highway without tolls or delays.
E. A person's sense of values, and having assets with below-market value.

3. A great way to solve a problem is to discover that it has already been solved. There may be an analogous problem with a known solution that you can apply to your problem. To find an analogous problem, you generally have to look for similar features or structures. For example, the problem of finding your way when walking through fog is analogous to a nearsighted person finding her way around without glasses; fog limits the visibility for people with normal eyes the way nearsightedness limits the visibility of those afflicted with it. This analogy suggests a solution for walking in the fog: special glasses or light that eliminates the visual distortion.

- Can you think of analogies to these problems that might suggest a solution?

    A. Not being able to start your car on cold mornings is like

    _____.

    B. Trying to rid your basement of mice is like _____.
    C. Overdrawing your checking account is like _____.
    D. Having an answering machine that can't hold all your messages is like _____.

Suggested analogies (yours will be different, and maybe better):

A. Like being too cold to do your morning exercises. A solution to the car problem, therefore, is warming it up (cover it the night before), which is like doing something to warm up before exercising.
B. Like trying to stop marbles rolling down a sidewalk. The marble solution is to make some kind of funnel trap for the marbles and thus a funnel-like trap—for instance, a food-lined cage—for the mice.
C. Like running out of toothpaste. A solution is to replenish both (toothpaste and checking account) before they're exhausted or to find new ways to "squeeze out" money, like arranging for a floating loan.

D. Like owning a trash can that's too small. A solution for both is to empty it more often or get something larger.

4. Discovering connections between common words is a useful exercise for learning how to form new connections. In turn, these connections sometimes produce new solutions to old problems. A student asked to find a connection between traffic lights and cigarettes came up with the idea of putting a red band around a cigarette close to the butt end to indicate that the smoker was about to puff on the most hazardous part of the cigarette.

- Here are pairs of random words. See if you can find a connection between each.

    A. Forest—milk
    B. Dentist—sailing
    C. Chain saw—pep talk
    D. College entrance exam—suspenders

    Possible answers (yours may be very different):

    A. **Forest**—maple trees—spouts draining sap for syrup—cow being milked—**milk**
    B. **Dentist**—crowns and root canal—numerous difficult procedures—sailing into the wind using many small tacks—**sailing**
    C. **Chain saw**—hedge trimming—winter garden cleanup—coercing teenager into pruning—**pep talk**
    D. **College entrance exam**—practice tests—flash cards—image of former teacher wearing **suspenders**

5. A group of air force colonels and majors was given this problem: "If 700 miles of outside telephone wire were coated with three inches of frost so that long-distance calls could not be made, how would you restore normal service as soon as possible?" The group produced 53 ideas

in 25 minutes. The best solution was to send helicopters to fly over the wires so that downdraft from their blades would quickly blow the frost off.

- Try to brainstorm solutions to these problems:

You are the marketing director of a company that makes toothbrushes. You have just learned that, through a manufacturing mistake, you have 50,000 surplus children's brushes. What uses can you market them for other than brushing teeth?

Possible answers: They can be marketed as jewelry cleaners or kitchen utensils ("clean the spots that are hard to reach"), or sold to shoe companies to be put in shoe boxes as small buffers.

What features in your home would be improved if they were curved instead of straight?

Possible answers: The corners on the dining room table; the plastic kitty-litter scoop, which regularly breaks; the television remote control, which often gets sandwiched into magazines or newspapers. If it were round and thick, it would be easier to spot.

Your dinner guests play with your children right before they go to bed, getting them too excited to sleep. What can you do to prevent this from happening again?

Possible answers: Ask the guests to read to the children instead of play. Put children to bed before guests think of going upstairs.

The U.S. Mint has twice created dollar coins, the Susan B. Anthony and the Sacagawea, then halted production because people weren't using them. The government has spent millions trying to get people to use dollar coins, which are cheaper to make in the long run than paper money and harder to counterfeit. Can you think of ways to get people to use dollar coins?

Possible answers: Offer an incentive to trade paper for coin, like a small tax break. Offer to exchange badly damaged paper bills for the coins. Make the coins much lighter. Realize that it's a losing battle and tell the Treasury to stop trying.

CHAPTER 8

Solving Problems

Now it's time to use your Intelligent Memory. Knowing how to pay attention, strengthen your scratch-pad memory, store more extensive memories, and extend connections all contribute to the raw material of Intelligent Memory but are only the means to an end. Intelligent Memory is best used for sparking new insights and coming up with creative ideas. It's especially good at finding solutions to a wide assortment of problems, as we touched on in the previous chapter.

THE NATURE OF PROBLEMS

A "problem" is the difference between where you are and where you want to be. It's a situation that needs improving. This can be any sort of situation, either physical or mental. A problem can be as simple as opening a stuck drawer and as complex as trying to resolve the conflict in the Middle East. It can be as emotionally charged as deciding who to marry and as mundane as finding enough time to do the laundry.

Problems are generally either well defined or ill defined. A well-defined problem has a clear goal, and everything you may need to reach the solution is at hand; you have all the ingredients and all the tools you need. You just have to apply them properly.

Math problems are perfect examples of well-defined problems.

What you are asked to solve is clear. You have all the ingredients—numbers—and you have all the tools—addition, subtraction, multiplication, and other math functions. Everything you can possibly do is written somewhere, even if you don't know it. The universe of possible solutions is relatively small. And even if you have to consider an assortment of formulas or numbers, you know that the solution will be in a certain domain of knowledge—that is, numbers. No one expects the solution to a math problem to be a Bronx cheer. This is why math problems appear so often in brainteaser or puzzle books; they have clear right or wrong answers, and are easy to describe and score.

We encounter well-defined problems every day, such as figuring out how much wallpaper we need for a new bathroom, fixing a jammed printer, comparing prices when shopping, or finding the quickest route to a new store. The goal is clear and we usually know how to get there.

Unfortunately, most of the problems we face in life, and almost all of the important ones, are ill defined. A problem is ill defined if its solution, information, or the mental tools you might use to solve it can't be easily identified. We are inundated by ill-defined problems: figuring the best way to save money or get a promotion, deciding what to give someone for Christmas, proposing a child-custody schedule, deciding what kind of Halloween costume to make for a child, deciding what to say in a sympathy note, or planning a surprise birthday party.

For example, one goal of many people is to be happy. But what really is the happiness that they seek? What material would anyone use to "make" happiness? What tools? Just what to do is very ill defined. It's well known that one way to make people happy is to make them miserable, then take the misery away. They'll be happy, at least for a while. Yet this seems to miss what people imagine when they hope for happiness. And even though people think they'll be happy if they win the lottery, studies of lottery winners have shown that most of them are no happier than they were before they won. But *not* winning the lottery seems to miss the point as well.

Our intention here is not to show you how to win the lottery, but to show you how to understand the problems you face. Understand the problem, and you've made an important step toward a solution or to deciding if a solution is even possible.

It's helpful to understand what goes on inside your head when you solve a problem so that you know where your Intelligent Memory comes in. Here's a well-defined problem: What is 1 + 1? First, you have to move the problem from paper to your brain. In doing this, you activate the Intelligent Memory elements standing for "one" and "one" and "plus." For most people, this pattern easily activates an answer. "One plus one" activates a minimind you learned long ago and connects to the answer "two." In everyday language, you've connected the dots. The pieces of the puzzle have fallen into place.

Now, the problem 1 + 1 = 2 is not very challenging, but does illustrate the basic way Intelligent Memory plays a role in solving problems. The minimind you have for "one plus one" connecting to "two" is so well practiced that it operated automatically, rapidly, and unconsciously.

These miniminds and connections are in everything, as we've seen. There are also miniminds that handle "word problems," although you may not think of them as problems anymore. For example, what is a four-legged animal that is a common pet and wags its tail? A dog. This too has elements ("four-legged," "animal," and so forth), an operator (the "and"), and connections to a solution—a dog. As with 1 + 1 = 2, these are by now automatic connections. You probably even had "dog" or "cat" in your mind just on reading the initial "four-legged animal," since that phrase has strong connections to dogs (and less strong connections, for most people, to horses or alligators or armadillos).

But now, to highlight more how the control systems for Intelligent Memory help find solutions, let's make the well-defined problem a little harder: What's "1776" "plus" "2001"? We chose this example because most Americans probably have "1776" as a unit in their minds. The number "2001" would be a unit as well, not just because of the new millennium and the year recently passed, but also perhaps because of the Stanley Kubrick movie of the same name. You don't have to create new elements to understand this problem, yet you don't have an automatic connection to the answer. Instead, you have to bring other miniminds into play. One minimind lines up the numbers:

$$1,776$$
$$+\ 2,001$$

and then calls on other miniminds to do the addition in the columns from right to left (6 plus 1, 7 plus 0, and so forth) and come up with the answer (3,777).

An important mental shift occurred in this example. Your Intelligent Memory could not automatically find the right minimind for an automatic answer, so the memory processing administrator took over. It identified a different minimind to cut the problem into smaller pieces and then fed those pieces into the same type of miniminds that you used for the "1 + 1" problem. (In this case, they were the miniminds for "6 + 1," "7 + 0," and "1 + 2.") You were still using your Intelligent Memory for addition, but it was being augmented by another set of intelligent memories, ones for breaking up arithmetic problems. There was a rapid shuttling process going on in your mind, cutting and pasting. You might dimly recall learning all these steps as a child, but now your awareness is most likely a blur.

Learning these steps is similar to what you went through learning to drive. But now, it's probably hard to feel the different miniminds that wake up when, for example, the driver ahead of you slams on his brakes. Having them in your mind has made you drive better, and having miniminds for arithmetic similarly allows you to better handle math problems. All problems are solved, and solved better, in exactly the same way when Intelligent Memory is prodded and expanded by the memory processing administrator.

What your mind does when it tries to find the right word for an object or concept that you know—that tip-of-the-tongue feeling—is the same process it goes through when solving problems. When you know the meaning of a word but can't bring it to mind—that is, when your Intelligent Memory doesn't automatically come up with the answer—its memory processing administrator takes control and tries to solve the problem two ways: It tries to find clues to help you search for the word, and it presents possible words to your mind to see if any fit the definition.

Here's an exercise to show you what it feels like to have missing or weak connections. Following are two lists—one of definitions and one of words corresponding to those definitions. These are words you probably know but also don't encounter regularly. As a result, the awareness of the words themselves and the connections to them will be weak, so there's a good chance your automatic Intelligent Memory won't give you an answer. Your memory processing administrator will go to work. You may be aware of the administrator trying to match the words to their definitions because the words and definitions will float around your head until it does. (To really test yourself, be sure to cover the word list and look at just one answer at a time.)

DEFINITIONS

1. A blood feud in which members of the family of a murdered person try to kill the murderer or members of his family.
2. A protecting charm worn to ward off evil spirits.
3. An old coin of Spain and South America.
4. A dark, hard, glassy volcanic rock.
5. A secretion from the sperm whale used in the manufacturer of perfume.
6. A building used for public worship by members of the Jewish faith.
7. An Egyptian ornament in the shape of a beetle.
8. The staff of Hermes, symbol of a physician or medical corps.
9. A sword with a short curved blade used by the Turks and Arabs.
10. A Russian sled drawn by three horses.

ANSWERS

1. vendetta
2. amulet
3. doubloon
4. obsidian

5. ambergris
6. synagogue
7. scarab
8. caduceus
9. scimitar
10. troika

There are several possible causes for a tip-of-the-tongue reaction. A word may have a weak representation in your mind, which often happens if the word is antiquated or derived from another language. It is also possible that the definitions prompted your memory to head down the wrong path as it looked for a word. This happens when the correct path is weak or nonexistent, and when other elements and paths (even the wrong ones) are strong. In this case, the strong-but-wrong word and pathway dominate your memory and you may find it hard to force your mind out of this channel. (One reason this happens is that even wrong connections get strengthened just by being activated.)

When your automatic memory looks in the wrong place, your processing administrator has to force your Intelligent Memory to probe elsewhere. It may have to suppress the strong-but-wrong words that get activated. You may even have to walk away from the definitions for a while to let all the activation die down so that you can try again.

All this happens when you solve well-defined problems, regardless of whether they involve one step or many steps. The arithmetic and word-definition problems, which are one-step problems, may take you only seconds to solve. Multistep problems can take minutes or hours because they have so many more steps. But the basic principles are the same for all, as is the role of Intelligent Memory, and especially of the memory processing administrator.

The process is the same for solving an ill-defined problem, except that nothing is clear and many options are open. Fortunately, this is exactly the situation in which Intelligent Memory excels. Intelligent Memory can keep many thoughts activated at once and rouse many connections simultaneously. However, too many possibilities are likely to jam the machinery or overshadow any solution that your mind may have found.

Thus, to solve any kind of problem, you need to beef up your Intelligent Memory, and its memory processing administrator, in several ways. First, your Intelligent Memory has to be well stocked with both thoughts and connections between those thoughts. If it does not have enough of them when you tackle a problem, be prepared to add them to your Intelligent Memory in the course of trying to solve the problem. This stocking process includes adding miniminds that can correctly process information.

For example, many people do not have miniminds that can handle basic statistics, even though we're bombarded with statistics every day. For example, when you hear "Fifty percent of doctors choose Easy-Off over the other leading brand!" how often do you think, "Well, that means 50 percent of doctors chose the other leading brand, which means there's really no difference"? A coin toss would have made an equally decisive choice.

The second requirement for solving problems is to narrow every part of the problem before you begin searching for an answer. Your memory processing administrator doesn't have infinite capacity, so you need to limit what it has to consider as much as possible. What information do you have? What tools or processes? The mushier the problem, the more dimensions it has, and so the more helpful it is to narrow your search for solutions.

One way to narrow the search is by setting forth your requirements for a solution. In choosing a Christmas gift, it may be a limit of $20 a gift; for the child-custody schedule, it may be an arrangement involving periods of seven days and no less. A requirement for the solution to the child's costume may be an outfit that doesn't require sewing.

Executives at an advertising agency faced an ill-defined problem when they were asked to create a campaign for the U.S. Air Force. At the outset, the possibilities for a campaign were endless, and the agency creative director recognized this. Only by narrowing the scope of the problem did they find a winning solution, which showed what the air force does by emphasizing its technology. The director further limited the problem, and likely solutions, by deciding that the ads would not contain any planes or air force staff. "We can't allow ourselves to default to the obvious," he told his team. The agency's winning ad showed an encounter between blue dots and green dots on a radar screen, with a voice-over saying, "The green dots don't know where the blue dots are. But the blue dots know exactly where the green dots are. . . . Poor green dots."

The danger in not narrowing or better defining a problem is that you pursue the wrong solution. You can spin your wheels with a useless solution or resort to a stop-gap solution, which only leads to the problem recurring.

Another requirement for solving problems is to be sure you are not too narrow in your thinking. This may seem to conflict with the second requirement—limiting what you deal with—and sometimes it does. However, these requirements are two aspects of the same thing. You shouldn't try to consider totally impossible conditions, but you shouldn't limit the problem so much that you're no longer dealing with the real problem. Nor do you want to limit the possibilities so much that you exclude possible solutions.

The French made this mistake after World War I. France had traditionally been invaded through the southern part of its eastern border, which stretches from Switzerland to the Mediterranean. To stop future invasions, the French built the Maginot Line of fortifications across the south at enormous cost in men and materials. The Maginot Line was a technical miracle, ultramodern and almost unassailable. However, in World War II, the Germans saw the problem it posed differently. They considered their real problem to be how to invade France, not how to conquer the Maginot Line. So they invaded France from the north, completely bypassing the line. Thus, you don't want possible solutions constrained by the past. You want to keep your options open.

This realization has dawned on some officials confronting today's open-ended problems stemming from an ingenious enemy. After September 11, 2001, the U.S. Army asked Hollywood movie scriptwriters, including the writers of *Die Hard* and *Air Force One,* to help it predict possible terrorist scenarios. When the risks are great, make sure you consider all the possibilities.

A more mundane example of rethinking the real problem comes from the experiences of a librarian who was trying to get children to read.

Reading aloud is a good way to learn reading, but the children in one school didn't want to read to one another because they were embarrassed about making mistakes, and they didn't want to read to an adult because they were intimidated by the adults' superior abilities. The librarian realized that all the children needed was to read aloud to an appreciative audience; the audience didn't actually have to understand what was being said to it. So she got the children to read aloud to dogs.

So, follow these strategic steps when you approach problems to help ensure that your Intelligent Memory will be used the best way:

First, understand the problem. What is being asked? What do you have to work with? You have to understand how much room you have, or how constrained you are.

Second, let your Intelligent Memory solve parts of the problem if it can't solve the whole problem at once. Let your memory process administrator help you break up the bigger problem into smaller pieces. This will eventually give you at least a plan for getting to the solution, if not an actual solution.

For each piece of the problem, let your Intelligent Memory and memory process administrator find the solution to that piece.

Repeat this process for each piece.

Finally, when you think you have a solution, run it through your mind. If it doesn't work (either in your mind or in practice), restart the process with the better understanding of what is necessary and what is possible.

Keep these steps in mind as you read about ways to make your Intelligent Memory and memory process administrator work better at solving problems.

LOOKING FOR SOLUTIONS

Sometimes solutions are already in your Intelligent Memory—these are the problems you solve on the fly. We may not even think of them as problems, since they're solved so effortlessly. For difficult problems, your Intelligent Memory may require a long time to stock possibilities and churn options before finding a good solution.

Charles Darwin struggled for years to reconcile what he saw on his voyage on the *Beagle* with what he knew about the nature of evolution. The prevailing beliefs in England in the 1830s contradicted what he knew and learned during his voyage. Nevertheless, the premise that formed his seminal work, *On the Origin of Species,* came to him in a flash while reading someone else's treatise on population. The solution to his ill-defined problem—how to accommodate seemingly contradictory theories of evolution, common ancestry, natural selection, and the power of reproduction—came from the sudden falling into place of his thoughts and knowledge in his Intelligent Memory.

Although considered one of the most important intellectual concepts of all time, evolution by natural selection occurred as a sudden insight to not just Darwin, but also to another naturalist, Alfred Russel Wallace, who knew nothing of Darwin's idea. While on an expedition, Wallace was forced to lie in his hammock each afternoon because of malarial fevers. During one feverish episode, he was thinking about how new species originated: "There suddenly flashed through my mind the idea of the survival of the fittest." What we can appreciate, from the perspective of Intelligent Memory, is that for both men, all it took was one more connection to solve the problem once most of the necessary ideas and connections were in place. The solution appeared in a flash although the preparation took years.

One of the greatest innovations in the sport of track and field came from the childhood memories of a teenage boy. Dick Fosbury was a high school athlete competing in the high jump and using the straddle method, which was used by all the winning high jumpers at the time. Nevertheless, Fosbury's performance with the straddle method was mediocre, so he wondered if he might do better jumping the way a child does, with a scissor kick. To accomplish this, he also had to adjust the way his body rotated and the angle at which he approached the bar. He discovered that his best jumps came when he sailed backward over the bar, following his shoulders. Fosbury's coach tried to dissuade him from his untested method, but the young man persisted. At the 1968 Olympics in Mexico City, the "Fosbury Flop" broke the world high-jump record at 7 feet, 4½ inches. Connection by connection, Fosbury saw his way to an innovative solution.

Necessity is the mother of invention because only then is our memory process administrator alerted to push the other parts of our Intelligent Memory to find solutions. When everything is going smoothly, our Intelligent Memory functions on automatic, even though this doesn't stretch it or create new miniminds to help us. Only when we are confronted by a new or vexing situation, or realize that the usual way of doing things is inadequate and ineffective, do we look for something different in our memory.

A friend's corkscrew dilemma at a picnic provides an illustration. Arriving early at the picnic carrying a basket that contained wine, corkscrew, and assorted plates, glasses, and silverware, she decided to have a glass of wine while she waited for her friends. As she was opening the bottle, the plastic corkscrew broke, leaving a metal shank in the cork and the cork still in the bottle. She had no other corkscrew. The shank was too small for her to grip to pull out. Her immediate thought was to break the glass neck of the bottle by whacking it against a rock. She knew that this would probably spill much of the wine and get broken glass into what was left. So she rummaged through her pockets and the picnic basket, looking for anything that might help. She wasn't quite sure exactly what she wanted, except that it had to help get the wine out of the bottle. She glanced at the car keys, bread knife, credit cards, eyeglasses, and silverware. When she saw the fork, her Intelligent Memory made the connection. In her mind's eye she saw that a tine of the fork could fit in the eyehole at the end of the metal shank on the broken corkscrew. She slipped the tine through the eyehole, turned the fork into a handle, and voilà—a perfect solution.

Admittedly, this is a trifling example of searching beyond the obvious. Still, this is how Intelligent Memory works for all problems, whether you're opening a wine bottle or discovering relativity.

LEARNING FROM LOOKING

Searching your memory for the unusual yet perfect solution gets better as you do it, regardless of whether you find one the first time you look.

Every time you look for a faint memory to solve a problem, you become better at looking. If your computer has crashed and you're trying to find out why, you learn new things about your hardware and software, and new facts and rules about how they function. Even if you never learn why it crashed, you'll know more the next time and do a better search for an answer.

Here are two problems to illustrate how trying to find memories that can solve a problem will prime your problem-solving abilities. The first is a textbook case of how problem solving can be primed:

> Two strings hang from the ceiling, one along the wall and the other near the middle of the room. Although close, neither is long enough to allow you to grab both to tie them together. Also in the room is a table, chair, pliers, paperweight, and coffee cup. The problem is to devise a way to tie the two strings together.

Psychology students trying to solve this problem first try an obvious solution. They use the chair and table to try to extend their reach. But the strings aren't long enough even for this. Most students get stuck at this point, so the teacher "accidentally" brushes against one of the strings, setting it into a swinging motion. For many students, this is the clue their Intelligent Memory needs to complete the circuit. They attach the pliers to one string, set it swinging, catch it at the top of its arc and tie it to the other string. Because the teacher's clue wasn't obvious, the connection it makes is unconscious. Many students who solve the problem only after the teacher starts the string swinging swear that they came up with the idea by themselves, but they didn't. Their Intelligent Memory made the connection.

Having read about that problem and how it can be solved, now see if your search for a solution is faster and more focused:

> On a table is a candle, book of matches, and a box of tacks. The problem is to devise a way to attach the candle to a wall so that it will burn upright.

Even if you can't figure out the solution, you probably realized that it involves using one of the objects in a way it wasn't intended. Your memory process administrator knows that it has to think differently than it might otherwise for these kinds of problems, and you expect it to. Having been primed for this kind of problem, you also retrieved and tested possible ideas more quickly than on the first one. While a solution—like melting wax from the candle to stand it on one side of the box and using the box as a shelf to tack to the wall—may have eluded you, you've improved your ability to search for a way of connecting what you have and what you need.

Successfully thinking through to a solution solidifies the memory of it and slows forgetting. You're less likely to forget a good solution, because by bringing it to the forefront of your mind, giving it your full attention, and connecting it with the reward of a job well done, you've strengthened all the memories that produced it. You've formed a new connection between the particulars of the problem and the solution, and will be able to tap into it at some future time. Your web of memories has become stronger and larger. If you came up with answers to either of these problems without help, you're more likely to remember them.

WAYS OF THINKING

Faced with a problem that doesn't solve itself, you need to think about ways of finding a solution. Ways of thinking that can help produce a solution are trusting hunches, deliberate creative thinking, using clues, and stringing together a chain of ideas.

When to Trust a Hunch

Sometimes you have a hunch that you've found the right memory. Hunches are often more than just guessing—they can be smart ideas. Hunches are the products of miniminds; they just aren't powerful enough to shout in our heads, so they whisper, and that whispering is called a hunch or intuition. Their feebleness may be due to several causes: The minimind may be brisk and decisive, but the information it's being fed may be weak or fuzzy, so what the minimind produces is enervated. Also, the minimind itself may be wooly, or it may be a thought sequence that is wrong but that you've never excised from your mind. Try this problem (even though it's a math problem, it really isn't about numbers):

> You are presented with two jars full of jelly beans. The first jar has 93 red beans and 7 white beans, and the second has 9 red beans and 1 white bean. You can win $10 if you draw a white bean without looking, but you must choose which jar to pick from first. How can you maximize your chances?

This problem has been tried on a number of students. Many select the jar with the 100 jelly beans "because they had a hunch." Their hunch was the minimind that most of us have that says "Bigger is better." Bigger *is* better much of the time, but not here. The odds of drawing a white bean are 7 out of 100 for the big jar. But they're 1 out of 10, or 10 out of 100, for the little jar. Those students who had miniminds that knew a bit of statistics, and could do a little math, were not swayed by the whispering minimind telling them to choose the bigger jar. We hope that if you picked wrong, you now have started creating a minimind more adept at statistics.

A correct hunch usually has some information, facts, or experience to recommend it. That's because it's coming from something inside your mind that has been successful enough for you in the past. There's guessing in choosing any solution—you can never know all the facts about a problem or situation. The promising hunch is the one that touches on an area that you know something about, even a little. This is what makes an expert a good "guesser." The doctor may not know what ails you but has a good hunch; the oil driller may not know where oil is buried but has a good hunch; the cop may not know who committed a crime but has a good hunch.

A hunch or feeling of knowing is more likely to be on target when the problem has a single solution rather than many possibilities. If you were asked, "Do you know the population of New Delhi?" and couldn't answer right away, your hunch of whether you could eventually find the answer would be fairly accurate. Most people know what they can retrieve from their memory. We know what we know—we may just not know it specifically.

When a problem extends beyond our knowledge, hunches are not as dependable. Sometimes we rely on hunches instead of thinking through a situation. We're especially inclined to fall back on hunches in situations that we think we've encountered before. Or we may depend on a hunch when we don't want to think too much, such as when we have to make a difficult financial decision or handle a sticky personal situation. When presented with a problem, your mind searches for the memory of a similar situation. It looks for a comparable event whose solution can be applied to what's before you. If it finds anything vaguely related, that triggers the hunch.

Here's an example of how we sometimes apply the memory of a similar but not identical situation to produce a hunch:

> Imagine that the Earth's surface has been completely smoothed so that the planet is a perfect sphere. A nonelastic string has been tied around the Earth's equator so that it fits snugly. Now imagine that the string has been untied, two meters have been added to its length, and it's been retied around the equator and distributed evenly around the globe. How much space between the string and the Earth's surface has this two meters added? Enough to slide in a sheet of paper? Your hand? A thick book? Is there enough space to crawl under?

You may have a hunch that the space is miniscule and large enough only to slide a finger under. Your hunch would be wrong. The space created is a little more than a foot, enough to crawl under. Your hunch may have been based on something you remember from geometry about small changes to large objects being barely detectable. You assumed that adding a few feet to a string around the circumference of the entire planet would hardly make a dent. While your knowledge of geometry is accurate, it is wrong in this case because it's considering volume, not circumference. When you add a small amount to a large volume, like a drop of rain into the ocean, change is undetectable. But the change in the radius of a sphere from enlarging the circumference is much greater and doesn't depend upon the radius of the sphere at all. The hunch based on similarity to volume was wrong.

Not all hunches are wrong. Many very smart, thoughtful people have arrived at wonderful discoveries inspired by hunches that bubbled to the surface after lengthy rumination—Einstein's theory of relativity and Darwin's ideas about evolution, to name two. It's the shoot-from-the-hip hunch that can lead us astray.

Beyond the Obvious

Jack Kilby was a young electrical engineer at Texas Instruments in the 1950s when engineers around the world were struggling to solve the problem of wiring electrical circuits. The problem was that any complex electrical equipment required miles of wiring to connect the parts. Everybody had been trying to solve the problem of too much wire by thinking of ways to compress the wiring. Kilby took a different tack. "I was the ignorant freshman in the field. I didn't know what everybody else considered impossible, so I didn't rule out anything," he says.

Kilby decided to eliminate the wires completely, and used germanium on which to imbed parts of the circuit, then carved channels in the germanium to act as wires. This way, he not only put everything on a smaller scale, but he was also able to work in three dimensions. Kilby's microchip revolutionized twentieth-century technology and earned him a Nobel Prize.

To dig into your memory and look beyond the obvious, you have to suppress the ideas that usually come to mind. In many respects, this is the essence of creative thinking—ignoring familiar thoughts and tapping into faint, distant memories. For creative people, this kind of thinking is so automatic they're unaware of the clichés they have discarded and how far they are from ordinary notions.

Another way to avoid an obvious thought and produce a creative one is to somehow alter the obvious idea. Add or subtract something. Change color. Change shape. Change size. Change design or function. Rearrange the parts. Use different materials. Consider its opposite. Jack Kilby changed the materials of electronic circuits, using germanium instead of copper.

Taking a lemon and making lemonade can also produce a creative solution. For decades, Ossining, New York, struggled to change its image, which had been colored for generations by the prison there, called Sing Sing. Civic leaders wanted to project the idea that Ossining was a nice small town to live in and raise children and to attract more business, but the presence of Sing Sing was a hard hurdle to overcome. So, recently, local leaders decided to start in a different way. They're now promoting their town as a tourist attraction, precisely because of the prison.

The English doctor Edward Jenner discovered the cure for smallpox by turning the problem around. Instead of studying those who got the disease, he examined people who did not. He noticed that dairymaids seemed to be immune from smallpox. However, they came down with cowpox, a harmless distant relative of the disease that produced similar-looking lesions. This led him to conclude that exposure to cowpox protected the girls from smallpox and led him to create the first vaccine.

Clues to a Solution

Finding a solution happens more quickly when you have a clue that points your thinking toward specific kinds of memories and ideas. Take this test to see how a clue can help you retrieve the right memory to answer a question. Read each sentence, spending a few seconds on each:

A brick can be used as a doorstop.
An orange can be used to play catch.
A bathtub can be used as a punch bowl.

A flashlight can be used to hold water.

A rug can be used as a bedspread.

A balloon can be used as a pillow.

A board can be used as a ruler.

A knife can be used to stir paint.

A guitar can be used as a canoe paddle.

Now cover the sentences and recall as many as possible. Most people can remember about half of them. With the sentences still covered, read the following list of clues and again try to recall the sentences:

Knife

Flashlight

Brick

Guitar

Bathtub

Rug

Balloon

Orange

Board

These words should have jiggled your memory, maybe even given you a brief "Aha" moment for remembering a sentence that you didn't earlier. That's what clues do—narrow your memory search and improve the likelihood of finding the right answer.

A clue is tied to the memory you're trying to recall. It can be tied in time—that is, if you hear or see a clue at the same time the memory is formed—or it can be tied through shared context, such as encountering a clue and an idea in the same situation or circumstances. A shared context may be an experience that's repeated: learning to dance in a certain room or memorizing dates in history with a study pal, and then being able to remember the right sequence of steps when in the same room or remember all the dates when you're with the same person. Product designers looking for ideas for improving shopping carts found clues by immersing themselves in the problem. They did this by visiting grocery stores and watching people trying to maneuver badly designed carts.

Sometimes, an emotional state can form the basis of a shared context. You may need to be in the same mood as when you first learned it. In this case, the mood becomes the clue. A study of the effects of alcohol on students shows how powerful state of mind can be as a clue. Students who learned while drunk were better able to recall the material when they were drunk again, not sober. The study also explains why someone who's drunk and hides money may not be able to find it when sober but may be able to find it during the next bender.

You may have to cast far and wide for clues if you're stuck for a creative solution. Although you will pick up lots of useless clues, and even ones that point you in the wrong direction, the more thoughts you stir up, the better the chances of hitting the right one. The director of creative strategy at Hallmark Cards throws a huge net in her search for ideas for new greeting cards. Most of her workdays are spent in her office in sedate Kansas City. When she wants other stimulation for new ideas, she goes on scouting trips to places full of energy and diversity, like New York City. In a single day, she may visit sixteen stores in Manhattan looking for clues and go home with two or three winning ideas to use in greeting cards.

Another way to find a clue that's going to solve your problem is to string together a series of smaller clues. By extrapolating from what you know about a possible solution, you assemble pieces of experience and knowledge and snippets of information that may prompt a solution. Take this wild example: You are trying to find out where rice is grown in the continental United States. The clues you start with come from your memory of the best growing conditions for rice—namely, flat land, lots of water, and warm temperatures. These clues narrow your search to the Southern states. Next, you review your memories of Southern states that are especially flat and wet. From here, you may well hit the answer—Louisiana.

Linking clues is a useful way of retrieving ideas and memories that you're not aware you possess. It can help you find solutions as well as deduce facts and uncover knowledge. See if you can catch the clues and answer this problem:

Two men are walking in a desert when they come across a mysterious dead man. He is wearing a small pack with water and food still in it, a larger but empty pack on his back, and a metal ring around his index finger. There are no tracks to be seen. The sand is smooth and undisturbed, no one is around, and they are miles from civilization. The hikers are baffled as to what killed the man.

They continue walking, and as they do, one of the men takes a handkerchief from his pocket but accidentally drops it. As he watches it drift to the ground, he realizes how the mystery man died.

Answer: The dead man had parachuted down. The parachute ring was still around the man's finger, although the parachute had blown away. The clue was the floating handkerchief, which triggered the connection.

CHECKING A SOLUTION

The best way to tell if the memories you use to solve a problem are the right ones is to see whether the problem is resolved. We often don't check results to everyday problems because we're accustomed to partial or temporary solutions. We go on diets that work for only a month. We make investments that decline in value. We tolerate household pets that tear up furniture. We set the alarm but are still late for work. But checking whether our solutions truly work is not only critical for getting right answers in the first place, it's also critical for making sure our intelligent memories are stocked with what they need to answer similar kinds of problems in the future.

Examining a bad solution can take you back to the beginning of a problem-solving strategy and force you to take another look at the problem. This was the position a swimsuit manufacturer was in when trying to design a suit that wouldn't fall apart or fade. The problem was especially knotty because few modern fabrics could hold their shape and color when assaulted by salty or chlorinated water. After unsuccessfully trying a number of synthetic materials, the manufacturer reconsidered the problem. It surveyed swimsuit wearers and discovered that 90 percent of suits never got wet. Women weren't wearing them for swimming but for sunning. The manufacturer now had a different, easier problem—designing a suit to withstand the sun instead of a harsh watery environment.

Sometimes we overlook the possibility that there may be a better solution and settle for an immediate goal just to get something out of the way. We fall into this trap whether the problem is well defined, like devising a way to stop a leak in the roof, or ill defined, like designing a better schedule for employees' vacation times. In either case, the best solution often begins with a better understanding of the problem.

Even the most open-ended problems can stand more scrutiny before you attempt a solution. The value of this approach was demonstrated in a study involving an art class in which students were asked to draw a still life of an assortment of objects. The students who produced the most creative work spent more time thinking about and rearranging the objects before they began and while they were drawing. They were constantly "problem finding" and searching for ideas on how to improve their drawings.

EXERCISES

1. These problems require you to search your areas of knowledge for the answer or to use a hunch. Can you tell the difference?

- Without lifting your pencil from the paper, can you join all four dots (on the following page) with two straight lines?

         o

              o

      o

              o

Answer: Unless you have direct knowledge of this kind of drawing problem or immediately see a solution, your answer is a hunch.

- You're in an office building waiting by a bank of six elevators. Do you know which door will open first? Can you answer this question using knowledge instead of a hunch?

Answer: Your answer will be a hunch unless you see an indicator among the bank of elevators telling you where they are in the building so that you can narrow your pick of which will open.

- Which city has a larger population, Sacramento, California, or Houston, Texas?

Answer: This question can be answered with either a deliberate search or a hunch. If you had a hunch that the larger city is Houston, it's correct and probably based on knowledge you didn't consciously think about. While you may not have known the populations of the cities, if you knew that Houston has more major-league sports teams than Sacramento and a larger airport, these facts steered your hunch in the right direction.

- For each group of three words, there is a fourth that can be paired with all of them. Do you know what it is?

Playing—Credit—Report
Board—Duck—Dollar

Answer: The right answers, card and bill, probably stem from knowledge. If you work with words, or are good at crossword puzzles or word games, you've got enough useful memories to know for sure.

2. In digging into memories for creative solutions, we're often distracted by conventional ideas. It can be hard to get beyond them to unusual ideas. This exercise will help you extend your memory retrieval to novel ideas.

- Imagine an everyday object and list all the conventional uses for it; then imagine an equal number of unconventional uses. For instance, if the object is a two-liter plastic bottle, conventional uses include: capturing rainwater, mixing orange juice, storing paper clips, storing leftover soup, mixing paint. Unconventional uses are: toy bowling pins, a flotation device, makeshift rolling pin, melted into glue, fish bowl, candle holder.
- Try this exercise with these objects: burned-out lightbulb, old tennis ball, CD jewel case.

3. To exercise your ability to link clues to find an answer, try these questions:

- Which wild animal can run as fast as a horse?

  skunk
  grizzly bear
  rhinoceros
  red ant

- In the seventeenth century in Europe, about 60 million people died from what disease?

  AIDS
  smallpox

    measles
    leukemia

- A brick wall and a plate glass window are both made principally of what ingredient?

    concrete
    graphite
    silicon
    sand

- Which plant can grow 3 feet in 24 hours?

    blue fescue grass
    oak tree
    bamboo
    sunflower

- Which is the largest organ in the human body?

    skin
    liver
    heart
    lungs

Answers: grizzly bear, smallpox, sand, bamboo, and skin. Even if you thought you knew nothing about these subjects, if you answered the questions correctly, you probably were able to stitch together enough facts for a good guess. The multiple-choice answers served as clues and helped you find the right information. In each case, the clues enabled you to think through the possibilities, review what you did know, and arrive at the logical answer. You retrieved knowledge about how animals move, what diseases do and when they appeared in history, building construction, what plants look like, and the size and shape of the human body.

4. This exercise tests how quickly clues can stimulate your Intelligent Memory.

- Here is a list of fifteen words that are clues to a single word that they all have in common. Cover the list and go down it one word at a time, spending no more than ten seconds on each. At what point on the list do you know the single-word solution?

    1. Times
    2. Inch
    3. Deal
    4. Corner
    5. Peg
    6. Head
    7. Dance
    8. Foot
    9. Person
    10. Town
    11. Math
    12. Four
    13. Block
    14. Table
    15. Box

Explanation: When a large group of people took this test, most of them found the answer, which is "square," at around the tenth clue. The terms are Times Square, square inch, square deal, square corner, square peg, square head, square dance, square foot, square person, town square, math square, four-square, square block, square table, and square box.

5. Each of these problems has more than one solution. Although they probably cover subjects that you're not familiar with, find a solution by using the clues provided.

When the city of London was building its subway system, water from the Thames began to leak into the hole that was to become Victoria Station. The engineers had to figure a way to stop the leak long enough to dig a tunnel and complete the station before cementing off the seeping water.

Possible solutions: Freeze the seeping water. Don't plug the seep but reroute the water.

The problem facing a city highway department was keeping teenagers from skateboarding in the smooth, concrete-lined drainage ditches. They didn't want the teens using the ditches for fear of liability lawsuits. They tried fencing the ditches but the kids went around the fences. They extended the fence but the kids cut a hole in it. They hung signs, but the kids ignored them.

Possible solutions: Lay ridges of concrete along the ditch so that they're unsuitable for skateboarding. Build a skateboard park nearby.

6. Here's a description of someone doing a number of peculiar things. However, there's one logical reason for all the actions. Can you figure out what it is?

Sally let loose a team of gophers. The plan backfired when a dog chased them away. She then threw a party but the guests failed to bring their motorcycles. Furthermore, her stereo system was not loud enough. Sally spent the next day looking for a "Peeping Tom" but was unable to find one in the Yellow Pages. Obscene phone calls gave her some hope until the number was changed. It was the installation of blinking neon lights across the street that finally did the trick.

Answer: Sally was trying to get an unpleasant neighbor to move.

7. For problems that seem unsolvable or for which available solutions don't work, rethink the problem. Try this approach:

A wealthy merchant had two sons who were both superior horsemen. However, they were very competitive, each constantly trying to outdo the other in equestrian skills. Their father grew so tired of their bickering that he offered them a contest to determine once and for all who was better. The winner of the contest would receive his entire fortune. The contest was a race from the family villa to a city 100 miles away. But there was a catch. The father stipulated that the winner would be the son whose horse finished last. The father wanted this to be a contest of their Intelligent Memories, not a contest of horses.

Each rider set off very slowly. After two days, they had barely traveled 100 yards. Not wanting the race to last for years, the boys' mother whispered advice to both of them. Soon after, they were both galloping toward the city. What did their mother say?

Answer: Their mother pointed out that the winner of the race would be the son whose horse that finished last, not the rider. So the sons swapped horses, each riding the other's. In this way, for the rider coming in first, his horse would be last.

CHAPTER 9

Working Creatively

Creativity is rooted in the same Intelligent Memory actions that you use to solve problems because it too arises from finding new connections. Most people think of creativity as something separate from what we do every day. This misconception comes from the popular belief that creativity is an exalted event or something both original and generally appreciated. Geniuses who produce wondrous discoveries and works of art, like Einstein and Picasso, certainly inspire this kind of belief. It's really part of the continuum of our mental lives.

Although such people's creative ideas fall at the extreme end of a spectrum, their creative process is not qualitatively different from what people do all the time. Creativity can be large or small, frequent or unique. Each of us does something creative every day of our lives. What makes our ideas creative is that they're unique and useful to us. When my older son was small, he got quite excited at having "invented" putting potato chips instead of ketchup on top of his hamburger. I was quite proud of him but gently explained that somewhere else in the world someone had probably done this already. Nevertheless, it was creative—original and useful—for him.

Another reason creativity is viewed as separate from what most of us do is that it's loudly trumpeted in the arts and most of us don't consider ourselves artists. Businesspeople and scientists don't usually claim to be creative; "creative accounting" even connotes disapproval, if not illegality. But whether it is artistic expression or everyday problem solving, a business problem or a scientific challenge, finding new connections produces a creative outcome.

Also, in the arts there is often not a specific problem to be solved. Instead, there is perhaps a goal. The goal might be to make both the viewer and the artist think about the profundities of life. It might be a way to appreciate beauty, or to shock our sensibilities. It might simply be a way to get us to laugh. Regardless of its goal, a work of art forces new connections inside the mind of anyone encountering it. This special quality of art—inspiring new connections in someone other than the creator—reinforces its dependence upon peoples' Intelligent Memory. To appreciate a work of art, you need Intelligent Memory.

MAKING GREAT LEAPS

Whether creativity is expressed in art or business or science, the basic element is a new connection between two ideas, or a new idea, or both. Your mind makes a new element, or finds something in common between elements that don't normally go together. A connection takes a leap into a totally new area, and finds a place to land. The longest and most unusual of these leaps are the creative ones. Your Intelligent Memory makes new connections all the time, either automatically or with the prodding and guidance of the memory process administrator. The connections that cover great mental distances generate creative thought.

The first step toward creativity is to establish the best spot from which your mind can jump. You start with what's in your Intelligent Memory, but you use any other stepping-stones to help you. It may take some time, and pressure, before your Intelligent Memory finds the right set of combinations. The process goes in fits and starts.

Then a connection is made, and when this happens, you feel it. At that moment, a whole web of connections is suddenly complete. A circuit gets closed. It may have taken months or years to piece it together, but when the last piece falls into place, the sudden rush of thoughts along the newly linked connections feels exactly like that, a rush. Alan Lightman, a highly creative physicist and novelist, has experienced creative moments in both fields and found that "the 'creative moment' feels the same in both professions . . . that luscious instant when an idea, or an insight, or an unorthodox understanding, suddenly gels."

INSIDE THE ARTISTIC MIND

A number of artists have described the process they go through. Interestingly, they emphasize the process more than their creation. They dwell on preparation and the searching process because those elements take the longest time. The following descriptions illustrate what these artists did to prepare and use the connections already in their Intelligent Memory to force new ones to sprout.

The Cartoonist

Jack Ziegler, a cartoonist, describes his creative efforts:

> If confronted with a blank sheet of paper, I go to that day's *New York Times* and scan the front page of each section, taking notes. If I have at least one thing written down . . . I can almost always get an idea out of it. I just keep fooling around, drawing odd bits here and there, until something starts to jell. Sometimes these . . . lead in a direction that has nothing at all to do with the word I wrote down in the first place and maybe I'm drawing and I sort of like what I'm doing.
>
> Sometimes I box myself into a corner and have to fight my way out, and all the while I'm thinking, Gee, I'd really like to fit this image into something I can use.
>
> If the *New York Times* fails me and there still is not a single note on my clipboard, I'm forced to revert to the hard discipline of daydreaming, a meandering that often leads nowhere but occasionally unearths a gem or two. I keep drawing and free-associating, letting one thing lead to another.
>
> Sometimes I find a groove and things start happening. I

stumble into one idea and that one leads to another. It's sort of an adrenaline rush that, after a while, peters out and, when I realize that there's nothing left, I gather these rough scribblings and stash them away.

The Writer

Stephen R. Donaldson, a celebrated science fiction and fantasy writer, describes how he works:

> A fair number of my best stories arise not from one idea, but from two. In these cases, one idea comes first; it excites me enough to stay with me; yet despite its apparent (to me) potential . . . it simply sits in my head—often for many years—saying over and over again, "*Look* at me, you idiot. If you just *looked* at me, you would know what to do with me."
>
> For example: the *Chronicles of Thomas Covenant* is squarely founded on two ideas: unbelief and leprosy. The notion of writing a fantasy about an unbeliever, a man who rejects the whole concept of fantasy, first came to me near the end of 1969. But the germ was dormant: no matter how I labored over it, I couldn't make it grow. Until I realized, in May of 1972, that my unbeliever should be a leper. As soon as those two ideas came together, my brain took fire. I spent the next three months feverishly taking notes, drawing maps, envisioning characters, studying the implications of unbelief and leprosy. Then I began writing.

Photographers and Painters

Writers have been the most articulate about the process they go through, but photographers, painters, and other artists use exactly the same process to find unusual elements or to make intriguing connections. Richard Avedon's arguably most famous photograph, *Dovima with Elephants, Cirque*

(Photograph by Richard Avedon. *Devima with Elephants, Cirque d'Hiver, Paris, France, August 1955.* © 1955 Richard Avedon.)

d'Hiver, Paris, France, 1955, is a dramatic example of familiar elements—a fashion model and elephants—combined in a unique way.

Photographer Cindy Sherman has described parts of the process in her diary. As with writers, it's one of fits and starts, trial and error, trying to find the right jumping place and the right landing: "I'm having a hard time finding a direction to move in. I guess I'm not inspired yet. I've been doing a lot of Polaroids of stuff I'm playing with. Perhaps that's keeping me from really concentrating, although I like the idea of it functioning like 'sketches.'"

Jackson Pollock, the abstract painter, was noted for his unusual methods and materials. As *Time* magazine observed, he "spread his canvases on the floor, dribbled paint, sand, and broken glass on them, smeared and scratched them. . . ." Pollock was trying to find new places in his Intelligent Memory to start from. He was also filmed and photographed at work, and can be seen pausing, pondering, then painting. The pauses, we can tell, are when the connections are being churned and when his mind is searching for just the right mark to make on the canvas. The process is the same for every artist and creative thinker; only the materials, methods, and goals are different.

LESSONS FOR MAKING CREATIVE CONNECTIONS

If you want your Intelligent Memory to find more creative ideas, you need to keep in mind several lessons from creative people, like those just mentioned who regularly and deliberately seek out new connections.

By its nature, a creative connection is very different from routine connections in your mind. If the creative connection could have been made from the familiar elements and well-trodden pathways in our minds, it would have been made already. So creative solutions need unusual elements and wild meanderings.

Since the elements and connections are unusual, you are most likely going to have to make them; they won't really already be there. Although you may have some already, you should expect to have to stock up on more from outside. They may come from listening to the news, or watching the patterns made by broken glass on a canvas.

This stocking process takes time and considerable effort, even though the effort may be accidental. Unfortunately, with creative ideas, you don't know in advance what is important to pay attention to and remember. Creative thinkers often try searching outside their areas to get fresh material and fresh insights. This can be intimidating but also exhilarating. Dashiell Hammett, the mystery writer, made it a point to read about everything, from religion to glass making to plasma physics. Steve Martin, the comedian, actor, screenwriter, playwright, and art collector, clearly draws on an extremely wide and deep knowledge of many topics to find humor and inspiration.

Expect many false alarms. These may be ideas that are perfectly fine but which fail to solve your problem or interest your audience in the slightest. Almost every creative thinker expects to have hundreds if not thousands of ideas for every one or two that actually prove worthwhile. While there's planning and purpose, there's also a great deal of trial and error, as shown here:

(© 1977 by Sidney Harris.)

Being creative and appreciating creativity both flow from a strong Intelligent Memory. They stretch the same mental muscles even though the creator usually has the much more uncertain task and therefore gets the greater exercise. Because creativity demands open-ended connections, the exercises for it are different than those in other chapters.

EXERCISES

1. What connections is your mind making as you read this cartoon? Which get stretched? What makes it funny?

"No, Thursday's out. How about never—is never good for you?"

(2003, The New Yorker Collection from cartoonbank.com. All rights reserved.)

Answer: We all certainly try to put off unwanted appointments as long as possible, but courtesy requires us to give some definite date. In this cartoon, the concept of a specific appointment time, but far in the future, is stretched by the time "never"—infinitely far in the future.

2. Try something totally outside your ordinary routine. Drive a different route. Set your radio on "scan" and listen to the strangest station that comes up. Watch a cable channel you normally skip over. Listen to a radio talk show by someone you've never heard of or can't stand. In each case, try to understand the perspective that went into the music or the opinion.

3. Browse with a view to stimulation and interest. Pick up a book on graphic design, particularly one aimed at stimulating ideas. Books out there for this purpose in the visual arts include Jim Krause's *Idea Index* (North Light Books, 2000) and McAlhone & Smart's *A Smile in the Mind: Witty Thinking in Graphic Design* (Phaidon, 1995). Advertising is a fertile source of creative ideas. One recent good sourcebook is Pricken's *Creative Advertising: Ideas and Techniques from the World's Best Campaigns* (Thames & Hudson, 2002).

4. Do nothing—daydream.

5. Daydream with a purpose. Give yourself a problem or a situation to think about, but spend time before tackling it to let your thoughts wander around the point.

6. There are a large number of useful compendiums of techniques to stimulate creative thinking. The techniques are all well known, such as trying new combinations, open-ended imagining, and brainstorming. An amusing sourcebook for such methods is Jack Foster's *How to Get Ideas* (Berrett-Koehler, 1996).

CHAPTER 10

Preventing Mental Mistakes

Intelligent Memory is not immune to mistakes. It's a collection of powerful mental tools—our miniminds—but the wrong miniminds may get called upon. Intelligent Memory may not have enough information about a problem, it may have the wrong information, or what information it does have may be too fuzzy to specify the right minimind for the problem. The miniminds themselves may be wrong, or two or more miniminds may conflict. Trying to force Intelligent Memory to work too quickly can lead to errors at any stage. And, of course, reality may not conform to what we think it is, or think it should be doing. Here are some of the problems with the way Intelligent Memory operates.

GENERALIZING TO A WRONG CONCLUSION

Intelligent Memory tends to generalize automatically, a necessity for our everyday lives. Generalization is a source of a great deal of creativity in our perception and our thinking. It allows similar ideas to get linked to each other. As we all know, however, generalizing can lead to mistakes. After all, not all traffic lights are the same and people don't look the same in different light. Sometimes generalizing can lead to leaps in the wrong direction or to highlighting the wrong similarities. When you started to learn to read, O and the Q looked alike and you were often confused. You learned to sharpen your perception to discriminate between them. There are many situations in our lives in which confusion is possible, but we don't always use caution.

The most dramatic of these occur in eyewitness accounts. Poor lighting, speed, unexpectedness, and fear can alter perception and memory for events. In one case, a man was accused of rape because the victim told the police that she got a good look at her attacker. She was positive that the man was the one who had raped her, identifying him in a lineup. In this case, however, the man had an ironclad alibi: He was giving a live television interview at the time of the rape. On closer questioning, the police learned that the victim had been watching the interview just before the attack. She had obviously blended his face with that of her attacker. The emotion of the experience had then branded his face into her mind as the one responsible.

FAULTY CONNECTIONS

Intelligent Memory may not make an important connection automatically because a connection may be weak and delayed. This is a common problem. We've all experienced the situation in which a good thought pops into mind too late to do us any good. Sometimes this has amusing consequences.

A night clerk devised an elegant plan to steal from the convenience store where he worked. He blocked the security cameras by putting tape over their lenses, then took the money from the cash registers and put it in the trash bin. He called the police to report an armed robbery, telling them that thieves had ordered him to tape over the camera lenses. He obviously expected to retrieve the money from the trash bin after the hubbub had died down. However, one connection that he didn't make was that you don't use transparent tape if you want to block a camera lens. The camera's videotape was a little fuzzy but clear enough to show that no one else was robbing the store.

Sometimes the failure to appreciate an otherwise obvious connection can have tragic consequences. Three maintenance men at an elementary school had sprayed cleaning solvent inside the janitorial closet.

One of them then lit a match, perhaps to sneak a smoke. The reason will never be known because the resulting explosion killed all three men and injured sixteen children. The maintenance men certainly knew that cleaning solvent was flammable and that an open flame could set it off but didn't make the connection in time.

Intelligent Memory soaks up experience, and this is generally a good thing. Everything you've seen, thought, or done has been saved in some fashion in Intelligent Memory, and nothing can erase that. The problem is that sometimes your own experience is not a good guide for the question you're posing to your Intelligent Memory. Your perspective may be too limited, your experiences too few.

Everyone's Intelligent Memory includes a collection of thoughts that they connect immediately. Some are as simple as "Stop if you see a red light" or "Run the other way if a large fierce animal with big teeth starts coming toward you." Connected thoughts function like miniminds—minds within our minds that are always churning as they link ideas and juggle problems beneath our conscious thoughts. While everyone is born with numerous miniminds, more develop as we gain knowledge and experience. The most complicated miniminds are created by experience and training. Examples include the weighing process that handicappers use to predict winning horses, the process a stock picker uses to identify good stocks for investment, or the strategies a golfer uses to pick the right golf club. More everyday examples are miniminds that think, "If something comes to mind readily, it must be important" and "If an event has happened the same way repeatedly, it will keep repeating until something changes it."

Miniminds are generally dormant until the right circumstances come along to activate them. A traffic light turning red activates a minimind that puts your foot on the brake without your even consciously thinking about it. In the same way, the racetrack handicapper, golf pro, or skilled crocheter may not even be aware of the thoughts that prompt her to pick a particular horse, golf club, or color of yarn.

There are two possible problems with these subconscious thought patterns, these miniminds. They may get called into operation when they shouldn't. Flashing a red light at a skilled driver evokes a reflex to put a foot on the brake, but not all flashing red lights mean halt. A lion roaring at us makes us jump, until we realize it's in a cage. At times, miniminds prompt us to do something or come up with a solution when the situation doesn't call for one. Making the situation worse, a flawed reaction or idea may stick in our minds so that we repeat the mistake.

Occasionally, miniminds are plain wrong. They may perceive danger where there isn't any or string together primitive or childlike thoughts that are part of our genetic heritage but not useful in modern life. Most people's reactions to harmless, nonthreatening snakes, an instant fight-or-flight instinct, is such a mistaken thought. Another example is the magical thinking that we all engage in at some time—such as the teenager driving recklessly because of his youthful sense of invulnerability and immortality.

THE VALUE OF SLOWER THINKING

Wrong ways of thinking get even more embedded in Intelligent Memory if they're not corrected. After all, what Intelligent Memory does well is remember. By itself, it can't know what is true or false, good sense or magical thinking. It records everything for later use.

Slowing your thinking is one way to stop your miniminds from generating erroneous thoughts. Your Intelligent Memory is fast, but it will do more if you let it work longer. It will be able to explore more of your network of ideas and associations, and be more likely to come up with the correct answer.

Not all thinking warrants deliberateness and careful attention, because the errors that may result are not consequential. If you slowed down to scrutinize every thought, you'd have a hard time getting anything done. Also, if Intelligent Memory generates an "Aha" insight, like a better way to paint your house, or a creative idea, like a novel approach to finding a better job, you don't need to rethink it. The new perspective itself is probably an improvement over what you typically come up with. Yet when the consequences are important and there is time, slowing down can pay off enormously.

Reading, for instance, is an activity that can benefit from slower thinking. Not all reading, of course—there's little reason to dwell over Sunday comics or romance novels—but there is reading that deserves more thought. Take instructions, which most of us breeze through. Slowing down for them can be useful. We can head off problems if we read the instructions carefully and work out the process in our heads so we understand what we need to do.

Imagine you have been asked to play a game for high stakes on TV. If you win, fame and fortune are yours. You read these instructions:

> This is a two-player game. Each player is given a deck of cards numbered 0 through 9. The cards are placed face-down in front of each player. Each player turns over the top card of his or her deck. If the sum of the two cards that are face up equals 10, they are removed from the table. If they do not equal 10, the player places the card back in the deck and shuffles it. The winner is the one with no cards left.

Simple enough, but if you read the instructions carefully, you'll realize that it is impossible to win this game. Since the card numbered 0 will never be combined with another card to total 10 and get removed from the deck, it will never be taken off the table. Therefore, there will always be at least one card on the table, the 0 card, and no one will be able to win by these rules. The game will go on forever.

Speedy thinking is a sign of intelligence. But smart thinkers also know when to go slow. When solving problems, smarter people think more slowly than others. They spend more time analyzing a problem and considering possible solutions. Studies of children considered "gifted" as well as successful college students show that they think more slowly when solving a problem than people who do less well. When reading new material, the good student takes more time, asks questions, and mentally organizes as he reads. Other students rush through new material and don't slow down for complicated or unfamiliar information.

Slower, smarter thinkers take time to recall similar problems they've encountered and solutions that worked. As they're thinking about a problem, they may restructure it—take it apart and think about its components—and envision it differently than at first. All the while, they're searching their memory for more information to help them solve it.

EXPECT FALLIBILITY

Your Intelligent Memory isn't infallible—no one's is. Nevertheless, many people believe that their ideas and logic are flawless. This is a common phenomenon, akin to the Lake Wobegon Effect. Lake Wobegon is the town where Garrison Keillor's radio program *Prairie Home Companion* originates. In Lake Wobegon, all the children are above-average.

At some time, we all have a distorted image of our mental processes. We think we're more insightful, more correct, more logical than the next person. Psychologists surveying teenagers and adults have found such mistaken beliefs to be widespread. A group of average high school students rated themselves as better than average at leadership, getting along with others, and writing. A typical group of business managers thought they were better-than-typical business managers. Many football players think that they have more "football sense" than other players. In one survey of people's understanding of their income, 19 percent of Americans thought their incomes were in the top 1 percent of the country. At least 95 percent of that group had to be wrong, and the other 5 percent could have been mistaken too.

People even think their sense of humor is better than others'. Students were given jokes that had been rated for funniness by professional comedians. After scoring the jokes, most of the students rated themselves as above-average in their ability to recognize what's funny. Even the students who thought this proven set of jokes was not very funny thought that their judgment was better than average.

As has been shown in other studies of accuracy, the students who were the most accurate in rating the jokes didn't think that they were. So one reason smarter people are smarter is that they are less sure of themselves, so they're more likely to double-check their answers.

THE PERILS OF PRESSURED THINKING

If we push Intelligent Memory too much, it can choke. Choking is well known in sports. Jana Novotna was playing at Wimbledon and holding a large lead in the deciding set when she became so concerned about losing and so painfully aware of herself that her strokes reverted to those of an earnest beginner. She lost the match. The major cause of choking—whether in athletics or elsewhere—seems to be conscious attention interfering with the smooth, automatic flow of a normal Intelligent Memory.

The possibility of choking exists whenever the stakes are high—when there's an audience, competition, rewards, or ego on the line. It can strike when you're put on the spot to perform, like a concert musician or an employee asked by his boss for a quick answer. It may happen while you're doing a crossword puzzle, helping a teen with homework, or even in tense driving situations. We may choke after we realize we've made a error because we're then seized with the possibility of repeating the error. The overwhelming fear that we will make another error makes us so self-conscious about what we're doing that any skill or expertise vanishes.

The solution to choking is, paradoxically, to accept errors in the same way that actors do. If you flub a line, forget about it and move on. Athletes ward off choking by talking about their fears and nerves. Problem solvers can ward it off by admitting the possibility of mistakes at the outset. Mistakes happen. They're even a necessary part of making progress. So accept them, and move on.

GOOD SOLUTION BUT WRONG MENTAL PROCESS

Sometimes we arrive at a great solution not from good memory connections or processing but coincidence. The investor who bought and sold Qualcomm the year it rose 1,000 percent needs to realize how much luck was involved. Did your air-conditioning unit miraculously start again after you jiggled a knob? Did your cold get better after you took vitamin C and now you swear by it? Did a bad thing happen to you when you parked in the high-rise lot and now you avoid using that parking lot when you have to go to an important place? We have to be wary of attributing every good solution or fortunate event to our Intelligent Memory. Often, it is just good fortune.

We might misinterpret a good result because we've confused correlation with cause—believing that because events or situations happened at the same time or close in time, they have a cause-and-effect relationship. We make this mistaken connection all the time: It's raining; there's a huge accident on the freeway, so we assume the rain caused the accident. We didn't get a raise at work and a new manager was just hired, so we assume the new person took our raise. We take a long flight and soon after get a bad cold, so we assume the cabin air and crowded plane caused it. Scientists are especially attuned to the hazards of confusing correlation with cause. When looking at how people respond to drugs, they don't immediately assume that if someone got worse, or better, that the drug they happened to be taking was the cause.

Another way that Intelligent Memory can slip is by producing a solution based on limited experience or giving too much weight to personal knowledge or experience. It's natural to discount information that comes from experiences we have not had ourselves. Nevertheless, this limited perspective can skew our Intelligent Memory, causing it to think that something is right without having all the facts and not knowing when it's wrong. This is why it's hard to convince a child to wear a bike helmet or a young person not to smoke. Nothing bad has ever happened to anyone they know from not wearing a helmet or from smoking. Therefore, it can't happen in their mind.

When I was an intern, I worked for a time in a cancer hospital. One of the clerks on the ward was a heavy cigarette smoker. He refused to look in anyone's room. As long as he didn't look, his intellectual understanding that smoking was the major cause of lung cancer didn't weigh very heavily on his Intelligent Memory. He knew that the moment he looked at the dying patients, he would have a far more potent memory to contend with. Of course, in a sense his Intelligent Memory was also correct, since not everyone who smokes develops cancer because of the smoking. But he was deliberately avoiding putting an emotional value on what knowledge he did have. A possibility may be rare, but too terrifying to accept.

APPLYING LIKELIHOOD AND ODDS

You are in Las Vegas playing roulette. The roulette wheel has 18 red pockets, 18 black pockets, and 2 green pockets. You've decided to bet on red pockets and so far, after ten spins, the ball has yet to land in a red pocket. What are the chances of the eleventh spin landing the ball in a red pocket?

Actually, the odds are the same for each spin of the wheel and determined by the portion of red, black, and green pockets. The chances of the ball landing in either red or green is 18 in 38 or a little less than 50 percent (this is why the house is usually the winner). This likelihood doesn't change no matter how many times you spin the wheel, or how many times any particular color has come up. Yet people are being misled by runs that are completely accidental all the time.

To see what you know about probability, try this one:

There are 40 people in a room. How likely is it that two of them will have the same birthday?

Actually, the odds of finding two people with the same birthday in a group of 40 are about 90 percent. They're so high because there are so many possibilities. This question is often used to show people how counterintuitive statistics can be. The odds increase rapidly because any pair of birthdays will do.

Our minds were not built to understand randomness or probability. We have to train them to understand the pervasiveness of randomness and how true probability works. Once we do, we will have added another powerful mental tool to our Intelligent Memory toolbox that will be useful in a wide range of modern-life situations.

Flawed probability thinking is believing that randomness has a pattern or logic. Known as gambler's fallacy, this reasoning figures that chance events are not truly "chance" but instead have to conform to a rule. It's thinking that after you've flipped ten heads in a row with a coin, the chances have improved for a tail to appear. The couple who has five sons and decides to have another child believing that the odds have improved for a girl are relying on the gambler's fallacy. Chance events do conform to rules, but they're the rules of chance. The gamblers who know those rules are the ones who actually make money (or make money by not betting at all).

Risks are misunderstood because we color our understanding with our fears. People have a fear of getting in the water on a tropical beach, but they're 15 times more likely to be killed by falling coconuts than by a shark. People in Africa are more likely to be killed by hippopotami than by lions. People eat more carcinogens in a hamburger that they've grilled themselves than they would ever accept in a product bought off the shelf.

TESTING CONCLUSIONS

Do you avoid testing your conclusions? A woman walks into a psychiatrist's office and says that she's a zombie. The doctor, trying to convince her otherwise, says, "You're walking and talking, aren't you?" The women replies, "Zombies walk and talk." The doctor says, "You're breathing too." And the woman notes, "So do zombies." The doctor considers, then asks, "Do zombies bleed?" The woman replies, empathically, no. So the doctor says, "All right, then I'm going to stick you with this needle and show you you're mistaken." He sticks in the needle and to the woman's amazement, blood begins to trickle from her arm. She turns to the doctor and declares, "I guess I was wrong—zombies do bleed."

There is a natural tendency to look for "evidence" that only confirms your first conclusion. This is called "confirmation bias." It can slip into your thinking in subtle ways: by asking leading questions when seeking information; by giving more weight to arguments that support yours; by ignoring facts that contradict or are counterintuitive to what you know; and by remembering only examples or instances that reinforce your beliefs.

In some situations, there is a natural check on the possibility for error because we get immediate feedback as to whether we did well or badly. Most sports, for instance, provide a reality check in their scoring. In solving problems and creative activities like writing or dance, there may not be an objective measuring stick. Or people may just not be willing to seek honest feedback.

So we have to devise ways of getting such feedback for our thinking. We have to be like the skilled thinkers who deliberately look for ways to refute their own conclusions. If they find such ways, then their conclusions must be wrong. If none can be found, then they can have more faith in their conclusions. Learning how to debate both sides of an issue is a good exercise for this type of thinking. Martin Gardner, a well-known essayist, wrote his autobiography and then, under a pseudonym, submitted a critical review of it. This was partly in jest, but it was also a very good exercise for a professional thinker to consider both sides of any issue, even his autobiography.

Nothing could convince the woman who thought she was a zombie that she was not. That's why she was considered delusional—no evidence would change her mind. Most people's thinking suffers from delusions that differ only in degree.

A man in Cedar Rapids, Iowa, broke into the apartment of a twenty-one-year-old woman. Sensing an opportunity, he awakened the woman and politely asked for sex. She declined, so the man asked for a date. She also passed on that. To get rid of him, she gave him her phone number and arranged a meeting. The man was arrested when he showed up for the "date." At his trial, his lawyer asked him, "Did you really think she wanted to see you again?" The man answered, "I didn't know for sure. That's why I came."

LISTENING TO COMMON SENSE

Sometimes the direct solution—the common sense solution—is better than the roundabout, clever, sophisticated solution. My father used to comment that there were some people who were so smart that it made them dumb about everyday things. This problem offers a good illustration.

> Working alone, Tom can mow his lawn in two hours. It takes his brother Dave four hours to mow the same lawn. If they work together, which answer is closest to the amount of time it will take?

> 4 hours
> 3 hours
> 2 hours
> 1 hour

If you answered three hours, think again. You chose the average time, but why would both boys working together take more time to mow the lawn than one by himself? Working together, they would have to be able to get the job done in less time than either could do alone. So the correct answer is one hour, at least of the choices given.

But one hour may not be the correct answer in the real world. This is where common sense comes in. What if Tom and Dave's family have only one mower? What if two people working at once make too much noise? What if Tom and Dave can't get along? What if they would get in each other's way? Although many hands make for light work, we know from experience that in some cases, they slow things down or make them impossible. One car mechanic can fix your engine but ten working on it won't necessarily make the work go faster. As many businesspeople have learned, throwing more people at a task may not accomplish more.

The litmus test for deciding whether you've used common sense is thinking about the practical applications of an idea or solution. Imagine yourself or others putting your solution into play or acting on an idea, then see if it still holds up. Another element of common sense is thinking about consequences. Undesirable, even disastrous consequences can flow from seemingly sensible ideas. A man in Toronto cleaning the bird feeder on his twenty-third-floor apartment used a chair to reach the feeder. However, the chair he chose had wheels. It rolled him to the railing and dumped him to his death.

RETHINKING A PROBLEM

Intelligent Memory sometimes tries to grab all of a problem at once or go for a knockout solution. Finding the best solution may require rethinking the problem or breaking it into subproblems that are easier to solve piece by piece.

Imagine it's two in the morning and your phone rings.

"I'd like to order a large pepperoni pizza," the voice announces.

"I'm sorry," you say, "you've got the wrong number," and hang up.

Three minutes later, the phone rings again. Same voice, "I'd like to order a pepperoni pizza." You snap at the caller, "This isn't a pizza place," and hang up.

A few minutes go by, and again the phone rings. "Is this Fat John's Pizza Joint?" you hear, slam the phone down, and wonder if you can get back to sleep.

Simple problem but the "solution" worked for only minutes. The real problem—the caller wasn't misdialing but believed that your number was the same as the pizza place's—hadn't been identified. Informing him that he had the wrong number did not solve the right problem.

The easiest way to pick apart a problem is to raise questions. Exactly which situation has been resolved or improved? Can you parcel the problem into pieces, each with perhaps its own remedy? Do you see a flaw with one of these subproblems? Have you created or solved others? Do you have enough information or knowledge for a solution? As a rule of thumb, it's easier to solve two small problems than one large one.

The problem of the divorced father offers an example. A recently divorced man wants to see his child more often than only weekends, but his ex-wife has custody. This problem has many elements or smaller problems: the man's relationship with his ex; the reason the man did not get custody; the child's relationship with its mother, and father; and the logistics of midweek visits. To solve this problem, the father may find it easier to think about the parts of it first. He may discover, for instance, that his ex objects to the extra visits for an easily remedied reason, like his not having a plan for how he and the child will spend the time.

Even problems that seem to have only one dimension can be picked apart. Consider this one: You're driving alone at night on a long stretch of highway that has little other traffic. You hear a funny noise, feel your car veering to one side, and pull onto the shoulder. You've got a flat and have no way to call for help, so you take the spare tire and jack from the trunk and start to change the tire. The night is dark and your only light is from a hazy moon and a tiny emergency flashlight. You carefully remove the tire's lug nuts and place them in the wheel cover. Suddenly, a speeding car whizzes by and scatters the wheel cover and lug nuts. Now you're in the dark, in the middle of nowhere with a flat tire, no way to find the lost nuts, and so no nuts to attach the spare with. On top of it all, it's beginning to rain. What do you do?

Although the main problem seems to be the flat, there is another: being stranded. So the solution you look for will depend on which problem you feel is more urgent. To solve the problem of being stranded you have a couple of possibilities: hike to a gas station, wait for another motorist to flag down, or drive to the nearest station on the flat, despite the damage it will do to the tire.

If you consider the flat to be the more urgent problem, you will look for ways to attach the spare. As you break down this problem and turn your focus to the lug nuts, a solution may come to you. You can remove a single lug nut from the three attached tires so that each tire has at least three nuts to secure it and you have three available nuts to attach the spare. This will hold it long enough for you to drive for help.

Another way to pick apart a problem is from the vantage point of a solution. Work backward from the solution to see if it really is a solution. Does the solution truly work? Does it postpone the problem or shove it to the back burner? Does it accomplish your original goal? Does it address the right problem?

The following solutions were proposed by entrepreneurs seeking venture capital funding. Can you suggest other possible solutions?

• The problem was how to protect homes in the West from forest fires. The proposed solution was a fireproof blanket that covered the entire house.

• The problem was how to share parting words and communicate final messages of someone who's deceased. The proposed solution was a talking tombstone—the final message would be recorded and then put in a microchip embedded in the headstone.

It's not that these proposals were wrong (although they didn't get funded). There may be better solutions, though, like using special shingles for the house near the forest, or keeping a tape of the deceased's final words for his loved ones.

We've given you a sampling of the mental mistakes that can detract from a well-functioning Intelligent Memory. By realizing that your Intelligent Memory may stumble or point you in the wrong direction and therefore through monitoring your solutions and conclusions, you can reduce mental errors before they become embedded in your memory.

EXERCISES

1. Connect the dots without raising your pencil and by using only four straight lines.

```
●   ●   ●

●   ●   ●

●   ●   ●
```

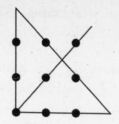

Explanation: As you can see, the solution requires you to draw outside the imaginary box, in short to break out of your mental boundary and functional fixedness.

2. Which of these poker hands is more likely to be dealt?

Ace hearts, king hearts, queen hearts, jack hearts, ten hearts
or
Ace spades, seven clubs, six clubs, queen diamonds, two spades

Explanation: Neither hand is more likely to be dealt. Dealing cards is random so you're just as likely to get a royal flush as a handful of nothing.

3. For each pair of events listed here, which is more likely to be the cause for someone's death?

Asthma—tornado
Bad cold—syphilis
Flood—homicide
Poisoning by vitamins—lightning
Diabetes—suicide

Explanation: Figures given are death rates per 100,000; the ones in boldface are the more likely. Are these what you expected?

Asthma—920. Tornado—44.
Bad cold—163. **Syphilis—200.**
Flood—100. **Homicide—9,200.**

Vitamin poisoning—.5. **Lightning—52.**
Diabetes—19,000. Suicide—12,000.

If you misjudged a number of these, it could be that your thinking was influenced by the wrong facts. News reports of unusual events, such as tornadoes, may mislead our Intelligent Memory into rating them as more prevalent than they are.

4. A town is served by two hospitals. In the larger hospital, about 45 babies are born each day. In the smaller hospital, about 15 babies are born each day. As most people know, the odds for girls or boys being born are 50-50, although the exact percentage varies from day to day. Some days more girls are born and on other days, it's vice versa. Over the course of a year, both hospitals reported that on more than 60 percent of the days, more girls than boys were born. During this time, which hospital do you think recorded more days of girls being born beyond 60 percent of the time, the larger hospital or the smaller one?

> *Explanation:* The smaller hospital. With fewer births, it is more likely to have days that violate the average. In a larger hospital with more births each day, the day-to-day variation in percentages is going to be smaller. This is often a reason for health scares. If two people come down with the same rare form of cancer in a small town, it may be just statistical fluctuation and coincidence, not poison in the water.

5. You're on a weight-loss program and having cottage cheese for lunch. The program allows you to have three-quarters of two-thirds of a cup of cottage cheese. Can you think of a mathematical way to determine how much this is? A practical way to measure it?

> *Math answer:* $\frac{3}{4} \times \frac{2}{3} = \frac{6}{12} = \frac{1}{2}$ cup
>
> or
>
> *Practical answer:* Form the two-thirds cup of cottage cheese into a round mound, divide it into fourths, remove one fourth and eat the rest.

6. What's wrong with this picture?

(TBWA/ESPAÑA)

Explanation: Nothing is really wrong with this picture, but your Intelligent Memory may have mistakenly "seen" the lion chasing the zebra. The picture violates our expectations of who should be chasing whom.

CHAPTER 11

Ideas for Using Intelligent Memory

You now know all about Intelligent Memory—what it is and what it does—but may wonder how to weave it into your daily life. It's not as hard as you may think—people do it every day but don't know it. Your thinking may be so quick and instinctive that you're unaware of all the memories and processes that went into a great idea.

To help you harness your Intelligent Memory, we offer examples of people using their Intelligent Memory at home, at work, and during leisure time. In each instance, they tapped into pieces of their memory, made new connections, and applied a unique combination of thought processes, like attention or an expanded scratch-pad memory, to arrive at their smart solution.

To best use your Intelligent Memory in everyday situations, you need to think about and do things a bit differently than you may have been. This means following such strategies as paying attention, making connections, looking beyond the first solution for a better one, breaking a problem into pieces, thinking twice about a hunch or taking many small steps to find a solution. These thought patterns are the ignition key for your Intelligent Memory engine—they get it started.

As you'll see, everyone engages their Intelligent Memory in a way unique to their personal abilities and situation. Just how you use it depends upon the memories, connections, and the mental processes that you've developed. One person may already be particularly good at finding analogies to help solve a problem while another may be adept at avoiding thinking errors and biases. Someone else may find it particularly easy to check their results. For each person, the route to a better Intelligent Memory is to devote more care to what they are not as good at.

The best first step for engaging your Intelligent Memory is to stop and think. Pause before you move forward with an idea or solution so that you can examine it a little longer; consider other possibilities; check the thinking and ideas that went into it; and review the result. Do this whenever the task matters to you, whether it's something important, like managing the family budget or something less crucial, like figuring a way to get your cat to stop scratching furniture. This alone— simply stopping to think—will exercise your Intelligent Memory.

AT HOME

A Teenager with Too Many Friends

It was holiday time and Gail's teenage daughter, Rachel, was in a fix. She had more than 30 friends and all were buying holiday gifts for one another, and Rachel didn't see how she could reciprocate. Many of her friends were from wealthy families and had much larger allowances and help from their parents in buying gifts. Although Rachel regularly earned money baby-sitting and doing odd jobs, she couldn't afford to buy gifts for everyone. And while Gail and her husband were certainly not poor, they couldn't afford to bankroll their daughter's desire to reciprocate with all her friends.

Gail picked apart the problem, breaking it into pieces and redefining elements. She wondered if it was really necessary for Rachel give each friend a gift. She redefined "gift" and suggested that Rachel might offer a group gift, like a party, or make a contribution to a charity in her friends' names. Another idea was to work the numbers and, given Rachel's modest gift fund, see if she could give each person an inexpensive but somehow personalized gift. Yet another idea was home-made gifts. Maybe Rachel could bake cookies or make candy for her friends.

Rachel rejected all of these ideas as either impractical or unsuitable. Time for more ideas. Gail returned to one of the elements of the problem: money. She considered ways Rachel could earn enough for 30 presents. Estimating a $20 minimum for each, they realized that such a solution was out of reach. While purchasing gifts was impractical, Gail decided that Rachel did have enough money to fashion home-made gifts. Rachel wasn't much of a cook but perhaps she could do something else.

Gail and Rachel stood in the teen's bedroom and scanned it for ideas. They saw and discarded numerous possibilities: hand-embroidered throw pillows, hand-drawn art for bulletin boards, tiny wind chimes for the doorway, candles. Gail looked at her daughter's computer and its features. The faint music coming from it inspired her. Rachel's computer included a drive that could burn new CDs. Rachel knew her friends' music tastes and that she could get free music off the Web legally. She decided to make CDs for her friends with a sampling of songs that they might like. The cost of such a gift was affordable, being only the cost of a blank CD. And it had the added appeal of being a gift that Rachel could personalize for each friend. Inspired by her mother's solution, Rachel began working on her holiday gifts. Gail's Intelligent Memory had prompted her to rethink the problem so that the possibilities expanded beyond the obvious or a first solution, like finding a way to buy 30-plus gifts, that wasn't very good. Next time, Rachel will solve the problem with her own improved Intelligent Memory.

An Inspired Fix

Professor Robert Weisberg, an expert on creativity, needed a solution immediately. While driving on an interstate, the power brakes in his car began to fail. Only by pressing hard on them was he able to stop. Unfortunately, he was a long way from professional help and he knew little about car engines. Fortunately, he was accustomed to solving problems.

Opening the hood, he immediately saw that a part of the master brake cylinder was gleaming white and hissing. The hiss stopped when he put his hand on the spot, and his hand was stuck there by suction. There was the problem—how could he find something strong enough, and small enough, to cover the spot? Wads of paper were too flimsy. He didn't have any spare metal lying around, and certainly nothing to cut a piece of metal to the right size. But putting his hand in his pocket, he felt coins and immediately made a connection between his requirements and a quarter he had. A quarter was strong metal, and just the right size. It solved his problem nicely until he could drive his car for a permanent repair.

Saving a Sentimental Keepsake

Heightened security measures around the country may make us feel safer but they can be inconvenient too. Kate, a driver in Washington, D.C., wasn't going to sacrifice a sentimental keepsake to the demands of absolute safety.

Kate needed to renew her driver's license and took the Metro, the District's subway, to the downtown offices of the Department of Motor Vehicles. As she entered the building, she encountered the usual screening routine: guards to search her purse and a metal detector to walk through. While looking through her purse, the guard found a small knife that she always carried. He informed her she could not enter the building with it. She asked the guard if he would hold on to it until she left the building, but he shook his head and pointed toward the door.

Kate was at a loss for what to do. The Swiss Army knife had been a gift from an old friend and she wasn't going to throw it away. On the DMV steps, she scanned the street and sidewalk, trying to decide what to do with her knife. The easiest solution—throw it in the trash—was unacceptable. She waited, hoping to see someone she knew to ask them to hold it. After a few minutes, she realized that idea wasn't going to pan out. Next, she thought about hiding it in the bushes alongside the steps then realized that someone might see her bury it or worse yet, think she was acting peculiarly and call a guard. Maybe she could cajole a stranger into holding it for her. Perhaps she could ask the hot dog vendor to keep it for her and buy a bottle of water to encourage his cooperation. Something about that solution didn't appeal to her.

She kept thinking, looking for a better solution. Her goal was to keep her knife so she needed a safe place close by where she could hide it. She thought about such a safe place—it had to be out of sight, preferably lockable, convenient, and cost little, if anything. Her eyes stopped on a coin-operated newspaper box and a connection snapped into place. Put the knife at the bottom of the stack of newspapers. She quickly double-checked the solution in her mind. The box was locked. When it was opened, people would only take papers from the top of the stack. The papers would not get sold out in the few hours she was in the DMV. She put a quarter in the box, extracted a newspaper, and slid her knife between two papers at the bottom of the stack. Two hours later when Kate emerged from the DMV with her new license, she spent another quarter on the newspaper box and retrieved her knife.

Cancer Scare

Understanding Intelligent Memory can help us evaluate the risks involved in important medical decisions. While some parts of our Intelligent Memory want to jump to conclusions, other parts can give us more reasoned, and usually more correct, answers. Having the right answer can be a matter of life or death.

During an annual physical, Beth, a thirty-nine-year-old woman, learned that she had a small lump in her breast. The doctor told her that given her age and medical history, the chance of the lump being cancerous was .05, in other words, 1 in 20. The doctor recommended that she have a mammogram. Beth asked what it would mean if the mammogram was abnormal. She also wondered whether it was still possible that she might have cancer even if the mammogram didn't show anything.

The doctor told her that among women like her who did have cancer, the disease was apparent 80 percent of the time on mammography. That is, the mammogram usually, but not always, detected it. However, the mammogram could also be wrong. Mammograms were positive about 20 percent of the time even when there was no cancer present.

Beth had the mammogram and it was positive. She left the mammography suite devastated, certain she had cancer. A friend, less emotionally involved, gave her a more accurate interpretation of what the statistics meant.

The friend gave Beth this example: consider 100 women like her who had an abnormal breast examination. One in 20 with abnormal breast examinations would actually have cancer, or 5 of the 100 women. If all those five women got mammograms, then the mammogram would be expected to be positive in 4 of the 5, and negative in 1 of the 5.

But of the original 100 women with abnormal breast examinations, 95 would not have breast cancer. Nineteen of these women would also have positive mammograms because of the false positive rate even though they didn't have cancer.

Therefore, with what was known of her condition so far, Beth's actual chance of having cancer was about 17 percent, not the near certainty she thought. That's because there were 23 women of the original group of 100 with positive mammograms (4 plus 19) but only 4 of these women actually had breast cancer. So the real odds for having breast cancer from all the tests at this point was 4 out of 23, or 17 percent. Beth still had more than an 80 percent chance of not having breast cancer, despite the lump in her breast and despite the abnormal mammogram.

Probabilities are tough for an untutored Intelligent Memory to deal with because they're often so counterintuitive. Our era of medical miracles is also an era of probabilities and possibilities so it's important to understand what an abnormal medical test may actually mean and how probabilities work, so you'll know if they're working for you or against you. It's also important to realize that a probability is not a certainty, it's only a chance.

Take Another Test?

Judy, a high school senior, was ecstatic. She had just received her college entrance test scores and they were far beyond what she or her teachers expected. Her combined scores had put her into the ninety-fifth percentile. When she had taken the test before, she had been in the eighty-fifth percentile. Judy's father was also delighted and reminded his daughter that he had predicted all along that she would do well on the test. He believed that her score was not an anomaly but an accurate indicator of her ability and wanted her to take the test again. He argued that she was on a roll and would probably do even better the next time.

Judy was torn: While an even higher score would be nice, what if the last score was a fluke and the next time she did worse? This is the kind of situation in which an Intelligent Memory familiar with probability can produce the best answer.

In this case, the answer came from her younger brother, whose young Intelligent Memory was well schooled in baseball statistics and probabilities. The brother was talking about his favorite baseball player, an outfielder who had had a terrific season, batting .310, and was being offered a big raise in his contract. The brother commented, "He better take the money now because he'll never again have a season like this one."

Judy asked why. "The law of averages," her brother said. "In the last five years, he's never batted over .280, so he'll probably sink back to that next year."

Judy realized that her high score might be like the player's one fabulous batting season. Her own track record was eighty-fifth percentile and ninety-fifth percentile. As much as she wanted to believe she could be better, it was most likely that her true ability was between the eighty-fifth and ninety-fifth percentile levels and she would score in this range if she took the test again. She could get lucky and do better the ninety-fifth percentile, but it was more likely that she would do worse. Knowing this, Judy was in a better position to decide whether to take the chance or not.

AT WORK

Managing a Grocery Store

A grocery store was losing customers because of its long checkout lines. People would shop, wait in line for a while, then become so annoyed that they abandoned their carts and left the store. The problem had been going on for so long that some shoppers weren't even going into the store. They'd peer through the windows, see the snaking lines, and go somewhere else. After a steady decline in sales, the store owners told the manager to find a quick, affordable solution.

Tim, the manager, began by studying the problem. For a couple of days, he watched the flow of customers and noted a number of possible reasons for the slow lines: Some cashiers were particularly slow, certain times of the day were busier than others, the number of checkout lines remained more or less constant, and some food items caused backups because they had no price labels.

Each of these smaller problems prompted a partial solution: Tim could train the cashiers to work faster. He could open more lines at busy times of the day, especially various types of express lines. Yet another idea was to designate an employee as a runner to check a price when there was a question. One more possibility was to upgrade the store's scanners for faster technology. All of these solutions were aimed at speeding the flow of people through the checkout lines.

Tim turned his thoughts to a new direction. Perhaps the problem stemmed not from the store but from the customers. Perhaps they were too slow and inefficient in their shopping. Maybe the customers needed training, or at least suggestions for how to move more quickly through a line. Yet another tack was to change customers' perception of the problem. By reducing people's impatience while they waited, the manager could minimize the problem in the customers' minds.

Tim decided to address both the store problem and the customer problem. He added more express lines at key times of the day and also found ways to entertain people while they were waited, like giving out food samples and arranging racks at the checkout counters to entice them to continue shopping. And he evened the flow of customers through the day by offering special sales and coupons for off-peak times.

Many business problems tend to be classic ill-defined problems with numerous variables, smaller problems within them and no absolute, right solution. Sometimes we look for a single, silver-bullet solution and don't think about numerous smaller ones. Yet with ill-defined, multidimensional problems, the best solution may be many solutions.

Getting a Better Job

Robert, an executive at a major automaker, had reached a breaking point. Even though he had had his job for many years, loved it, and the pay and perks were excellent, he loathed his boss. Over the years, he had tried all kinds of ways to improve the situation. He transferred to another department but later had to return to his old position. He arranged his hours so he'd be around the boss as little as possible. Nevertheless, as the executive's responsibilities grew, so did his contact with the odious boss. He'd had enough and planned to quit. He contacted a headhunter to find another position within the industry first.

Fortunately, Robert told his wife about his plans. She pointed out to him that while his problem with his boss would be solved if he left his job, his problem would also get solved if his boss left. That might be an even better solution because then Robert might be promoted within the job he loved.

Of course, the jobs Robert had asked the headhunter to find him were the same kinds of jobs his boss would be qualified for. The next day, Robert called the headhunter, withdrew his name, and gave the man his boss's name. When the headhunter called the boss to see if he would be interested in a position elsewhere, the man said he had been thinking about leaving. The executive's problem was solved with his boss's exit.

This is a classic example of rethinking the actual problem. Often, just reconsidering what the problem really is points a way to a solution.

Smart Trash

Trash collection in Tallahassee, Florida, used to require picking up trash cans once a week from each home, emptying them into a truck, then taking them back to the house. Each pickup required two trips—one to get the trash can, the second to return it. This made it very labor intensive. Most of the employees were young men right out of high school. The work was hard and hot, and there was constant turnover on the crews. This was the way it had always been done, so the notion of improving it didn't seem to have occurred to anyone until an older man—we'll call him George—joined one of the crews.

George hauled trash cans back and forth like everyone else, and encountered the same facts about the job as everyone else. One fact was that the city, not the home owners, owned the trash cans. Another was that the trash cans all looked the same. Home owners did not personalize their trash cans since the city owned them all.

George then made a connection between these facts that others had not. Since every trash can was identical, there was no need to return the original can to each house. A house could be given any empty trash can. Knowing this, George could walk into a yard with an empty trash can from the prior house, pick up the full can, take it back to the truck, and then take that empty one to the next house. The only extra work was at the end of the day when an empty trash can had to go back to the first house on the route. With this insight, George cut the number of trips the crews made in half.

George's idea didn't require any new facts for his Intelligent Memory. It used known facts to make new connections. Everyone knew that the trash cans were owned by the city and that they were all the same. No one thought the home owners had special relationships with their trash cans. And no one liked walking back and forth twice to each house in the Florida heat. But everyone else did it without wondering if there was a better way, and without trying to think about a better way.

Perhaps George thought about the problem because he was older and less interested in using his muscles than the young men. Perhaps he was more accustomed to questioning authority. What is clear is that he used his Intelligent Memory by asking if the job could be done better, then searched among the facts and possibilities for shortcuts and better methods. Once he thought about it, the new connections delivered the shortcut.

An Inspiration from Childhood

James F. Bradley Jr. was a captain in the navy assigned to a military intelligence unit when he came up with an idea that gave the United

States a huge advantage over the Soviet Union during the Cold War. It was 1970, and the Soviets were using underwater cables to communicate with their submarine and navy fleet. The United States had been looking for ways to intercept these communications but were stymied because they could not locate the underwater cables.

Bradley's inspiration came at 3 A.M. when he was still at the office and thinking about ways to enhance the intelligence information the navy was gathering. He let his mind wander, perhaps doing a little personal brainstorming. He pictured underwater cables and then remembered growing up along the banks of the Mississippi River, where there were numerous signs warning, "Cable Crossing—Do Not Anchor." He wondered if the Soviets had similar signs in areas where their cables disappeared from the land into the water.

He contacted someone familiar with the Soviet coastline to check his theory. In 1971, the American submarine *Halibut* slowly approached the Siberian coast, its periscope up. Sure enough, it spotted warning signs. From there, the navy located the cables and followed them into the Sea of Okhotsk, where it attached an intercept. For the next nine years, the U.S. Navy was privy to all sorts of Soviet communications, including some from its Northern Fleet and its intelligence agency.

The Boss Who Stayed Late

It was well past 5 P.M., and while the reception area was dark, many individual offices as well as the boss's corner office were bright. As usual, the boss was still in his office and so his employees were in their offices, but not because they wanted to be. Ambitious employees or even employees not wanting to draw attention to themselves stayed on because they didn't want to be seen as less dedicated than the boss. This situation was causing considerable resentment. Employees felt forced into staying late for no good reason other than appearances.

The senior manager knew the situation and how unhappy people were, but he didn't know what to do about it. With employees' energy and morale sinking, he had to solve the problem and so considered possible solutions. He could order the employees to go home. He could tell them to show up later in the mornings so that their after-hours time was not excessive. He could assign them more work and give comp time for the effort. There was yet an entirely different tack he could take—he could change the boss's behavior.

Since the manager couldn't order the boss to go home, he decided to learn more about why the boss always stayed late. One evening the senior manger stopped in the boss's office and saw him with his feet on the desk, reading a newspaper and watching TV. This was not what the senior manager expected to see. The boss was relaxed and obviously not devoting his after-hours to business. The manager wondered aloud why his boss was at work so late. The boss confessed that he had six kids at home and this was his only chance to unwind and catch up on the news. It was probably at this moment that the solution came to the senior manager.

He asked his boss to accompany him on a walk through the company's offices. As they walked, they stopped at every office where other people were also staying late. Most of the employees looked only semi-busy. They were reading, filing, updating records. After the tour, the senior manager pointed out to the boss that the only reason these people were still at the office was because of him. This surprised him. He had no idea that his late hours had been sending a signal to his employees. He didn't realize that his employees had interpreted his winding-down time as a signal that they too must put in long hours.

At the next staff meeting, the boss explained to the employees why he stayed late. He told them about his family and the chaos with all the kids and how much he enjoyed quiet time to read the paper. Most important, he told them to stop putting in long days and to go home at the normal time. He knew they worked hard during the day and wanted them to get the personal time and rest that they needed. With considerable relief, this is exactly what people did. Problem solved.

Soaking Up a New Idea

Ed Lowe wanted to expand his family business, a supply company, in Michigan. He sold sawdust as an industrial absorbent, but he didn't have many customers for it because it was flammable. Sawdust on a greasy factory floor often added to the fire danger. In addition to sawdust, he also sold kiln-dried clay as an absorbent for spilled oil and grease. He had tried to sell it to chicken farmers as clean nesting material, but it didn't catch on, so when a neighbor complained that the sawdust in the cat's litter box froze in the winter, Lowe tried something new. He sold her a bag of dried clay to mix with the sawdust. The neighbor returned the next week for more clay and sawdust and raved about it to her cat-owner friends. Lowe sensed a market, bagged more clay, and labeled it "kitty litter."

Kitty litter was a great idea, but it wasn't an immediate hit. At first, bags of it languished unsold, so Lowe told pet shop owners to give it away, hoping free samples might hook people. He traveled around the country attending cat shows and visiting pet shops, talking up kitty litter. Lowe eventually sold his kitty litter company for $200 million.

Intelligent Memory can give the inspiration, but getting an idea to actually be successful is still 99 percent perspiration, as Edison so famously remarked.

From Toys to Art

Alexander Calder was always clever with his hands even as a child. He used wire to make toys and jewelry for his sister's dolls and gadgets for himself. His mechanical bent led him to study engineering. He didn't stay with engineering, though, and soon after graduating enrolled in drawing classes and worked in various freelance assignments. An early assignment required him to attend the circus and draw pictures of circus scenes for publication.

Combining his experience with the circus with his skill at making wire toys, Calder first sculpted a wire rooster. From here, he expanded his universe of sculpture ideas to circus performers made from wire.

The next evolution in Calder's thinking was again a combination of connections, this time linking wire sculptures and toys. He had designed action toys that moved easily and were so appealing that a New York gallery exhibited them. At the same time, the gallery also happened to have an exhibit of mechanical birds in cages. Seeing this, he combined his action toys with the notion of fluttering birds to create his first moving sculpture, which he later dubbed mobiles.

Calder's concept of mobiles continued to expand. He experimented with scale, making very small ones and very large ones. This is where another set of memories influenced his thinking. The paintings of Piet Mondrian were large and abstract, often composed of rectangular blocks painted in strong colors. Calder was struck by Mondrian's color blocks and felt they should be put in motion. With Mondrian's influence, it was a short leap to Calder's trademark work—huge, metal pieces of geometric shapes that twist in the breeze. Today his sculptures are showcased in the world's most famous galleries, like the East Wing of the National Gallery of Art in Washington, D.C.

Calder's development as an artist is a classic story of building on ideas and networks of connections, drawing from memories and acquiring new ones to produce works of art renowned for their inventiveness.

Finding Gold

Tommy Thompson was a young engineer who loved taking things apart, discovering what made them run, and putting them back together. Growing up, he had two dreams: to be an inventor and to be an ocean engineer. After studying at Ohio State University, he joined the crew of a boat servicing deep-sea divers who worked with the famous treasure hunter Mel Fisher. Thompson never stopped educating himself, applying his endless curiosity and insight to oceanography, computer science, and robotics. He stuffed his Intelligent Memory with pieces of information that he sensed he'd someday be able to use.

His stint with Mel Fisher coupled with his experiences at sea led him to become a treasure hunter and discover the world's greatest sunken treasure. Hundreds of millions of dollars of gold had sunk with the SS *Central America* off the Carolinas as it was returning from the California gold fields in 1857. Much of the gold of the SS *Central America* was in the form of mint-condition double-eagle gold coins. These coins had never been circulated—they were perfect, museum quality, which enhanced their value. However, they had to stay in mint condition to be most valuable. A single nick would cut their value by a third.

The gold coins sat on the ocean floor 2,000 feet below the surface. It was too deep for divers and only underwater robots could function at such depths. Yet robots scooping up the coins were sure to damage many of them.

Thompson and another engineer distilled their treasure problem to its most simple elements: moving a large mass that was far away and consisted of many small parts without moving any of the parts.

They thought about a way to securely wrap the stacks of coins and came up with the idea of a mold, like a rubber block. This idea led them to a solution for how to get the coins up to the surface. They injected liquid silicon gel over the piles of coins and when the gel hardened from the cold water, they then lifted the solid mass in one piece to the surface. In this way, they brought up thousands of double-eagle coins in perfect condition.

A Quicker Way to Gas Up

Companies and marketers are always looking to solve problems we don't know we have. They make products better or more convenient to increases sales and the bottom line. With these goals in mind, the oil giant ExxonMobil began to explore simpler ways for people to buy its gasoline. If its gas were easier to buy, customers would be pleased and the company would sell more.

Company marketing executives examined many aspects of the process of pumping and buying gas. They wanted to make paying for gas more convenient and began to collect ideas. They met with people from Texas Instruments and learned that there were scanner systems and radio-frequency transponders that could carry customer and purchase information. They also learned that the tiny transponders could be embedded in almost anything and could be scanned.

The marketers turned to the mechanics of the transaction. They narrowed their ideas to three possibilities: a plastic wallet card, a car-mounted tag, and a key fob.

They asked questions like "How easy is it to withdraw a special card from a wallet?" and "How would customers feel about having a transponder attached to their cars?" and "What would be the best size and shape for a fob?"

Consumer research narrowed their choices. Customers wouldn't like the toll-tag method of paying because they're not physically involved with it. Wallet-sized cards are readily fumbled and lost. Something that attached to car keys would be best, since car keys have to be with anyone pumping gas into their car.

By reshaping, refining, testing, and eliminating ideas, they came up with a breakthrough in marketing—the SpeedPass. It's a 1½-inch piece of plastic with a hole through it for slipping onto a key chain. It carries credit card information about its owner, who has only to wave it at a scanner at the gas pump in order to buy a tank of gas. The SpeedPass notion helped spawn a number of other companies that offer small but always available tags for key chains.

Helping a Movie Star Cope with Pain

Brian Grazer is a successful movie producer, having made such blockbusters as *Apollo 13, Splash,* and *The Grinch,* and by necessity a good problem solver. The problems facing a movie producer include finding and recruiting writers, selling ideas to get movies financed, and keeping stars happy. One of Glazer's regular challenges is to keep stars content so that a production stays on schedule and on budget.

He encountered just this problem during the shooting of the movie *The Grinch,* which starred Jim Carrey. To play the Grinch, Carrey had to wear an elaborate costume and extensive makeup for many hours a day. The costume included thick, uncomfortable yellow contact lenses that Carrey found painful to wear. To solve the problem of Carrey's discomfort, and the possible future problem of losing his star, Grazer visited the set daily to talk to Carrey. He hired entertainers to keep Carrey amused and distracted between takes, so that he would keep wearing the contacts. The lenses still hurt.

Grazer decided that the thick yellow lenses had to stay. Carrey had to stay too—he was a great Grinch. Since Grazer was out of ideas for distracting Carrey from the pain, he realized that the pain would continue. Therefore, he had to find a way to help Carrey tolerate the pain.

The idea of being in constant pain led Grazer to the idea of torture and the question of what people have learned about tolerating extreme discomfort. He thought about who is actually trained to deal with torture. Grazer hired a former Navy SEAL, an expert in torture, to teach Jim Carrey ways of dealing with the pain. *The Grinch* was made with Carrey wearing the painful yellow lenses.

AT LEISURE

Traffic Jam in the Changing Room

Outside the fitting room of a large department store, a line of women waited impatiently. It was a busy scene largely because no one was allowed into a changing room until Stacey, the monitor, had counted each garment someone wanted to try on and had given that person a plastic tag matching the number of garments. The plastic tags were kept on a board by the changing room. This was the way the store prevented items from "disappearing" while they were being tried on. Store policy was strict. No one could go into the changing rooms without the right tag for the number of items she was carrying.

However, Stacey had run into a problem and the line had halted. The shopper standing in front of the line had only one item to try on and all the number one tags had been taken already. Stacey could not find a plastic tag with a number one on it. There were plenty of tags for twos and threes and more, but none for one item. Stacey searched in drawers, looked in empty changing rooms, and dug through a pile of hangers. She couldn't find a number one tag, and so everyone waited.

The customer seemed as baffled as Stacey as to how to solve this logjam. So they waited for someone to come out of the changing rooms and kept searching.

As the line grew longer, women began to complain loudly. At last, the next woman in line solved the dilemma. The woman walked to a rack where women put things they had tried on but didn't want to buy. She took a random blouse and handed it to the woman with the single item. Now that the woman waiting had two items, Stacey gave her a tag for two items from the board, and the customer disappeared into a changing room. Order was restored.

Both Stacey and the customer with the single item had been stuck in a mental rut. They were stuck on a rule: One garment meant a number one tag. Since there was no number one tag on the board, they were stymied. The woman who came up with the solution thought about the problem in reverse. There was a number two tag on the board. The answer, therefore, was to find a way to give the customer another garment, so she'd have two.

The Noisy Apartment

Apartments that house college students are notorious for their noise and commotion, but that doesn't make it any easier to tolerate music blasting at all hours. And if a building doesn't have a residence manager to help keep things quiet, residents are left to their own devices when a neighbor turns up the volume.

Emily was a serious graduate student more interested in finishing her work than partying or passing the time with friends. So when someone moved in below her who listened to loud music day and night, she was severely annoyed. What made the situation intolerable was that the music continued after Emily wanted to get to sleep.

Her first idea for improving the situation was to let her neighbor know that the music was annoying her. She pounded on the floor when the volume rose. This only slightly toned down the noise and not enough to restore quiet. Emily next attacked the problem directly. She marched to the apartment and asked the woman to turn it down. To her astonishment, the neighbor told her that she had every right to listen to music whenever she wanted. Clearly, ordinary solutions were not going to work.

Emily broadened her ideas for a solution. Since persuasion was not going to work, some kind of force was a possibility. Emily herself had little leverage but maybe the landlord or police could help. Emily complained to the landlord. The noise stopped. But within two weeks, it started up again, and the landlord was beginning to avoid her calls. A call to the police brought a half-hearted response.

Emily thought about drowning out the neighbor's noise with noise of her own, but then the neighbors might complain about her. So she next wondered about how she could change her noisy neighbor's behavior.

She then realized that her neighbor's apartment had the same layout as hers and that her floor was her neighbor's ceiling. This gave Emily a practical, effective solution. She bought a jump rope, set her alarm clock, and every morning at 4 A.M. jumped rope in her bedroom for thirty minutes. Of course, she knew that her bedroom was directly over her neighbor's bedroom. Emily jumped rope every morning for a week, until the neighbor showed up at her door to declare a truce. Emily agreed to stop jumping rope in the early morning and the neighbor agreed to turn down her music after 11 P.M.

Emily's experience shows how Intelligent Memory processing—retrieving bits of information from memory, like the jump rope, and making new connections, like between her floor and the neighbor's ceiling, and expanding upon and testing the new ideas—can produce a perfect solution to a multidimensional problem.

Equal Time

Bruce Vincent was the president of the League of Rural Voters in Montana when he was asked to speak to a class of urban middle-school children about logging, forestry, and caring for natural resources. He gave a lively talk about what loggers do and how forests are tended. As he was leaving the classroom, the teacher thanked him and mentioned that the next day an environmentalist was coming. The environmentalist wasn't giving just a talk, he was also arranging for the children to "adopt" a wolf.

Vincent immediately realized that the adopt-a-wolf idea was going to upstage his talk. "I wondered if everything I'd told those kids was out the window. If they were told that logging would hurt Alfred the Wolf, they'd forget everything I said," he reflected.

He wondered what he could say or do that could compare with the environmentalist's talk. He brainstormed. "Then it hit me. The only thing even more interesting than an animal is a human," he said. He came up with the idea of "adopting" a person, which evolved into a program Vincent today calls Provider Pals.

Under this program, 125 middle-school classes "adopt" a logger, fisherman, miner, farmer, or rancher. Through videos, letters, photos, and e-mails, the children learn about their person and his work. Once a year, a class's pal visits them and brings along interesting tools of his trade, like pans used to mine gold, and ropes to lasso cows. One pal even hauled a full-sized log to a class and cut slices for the children. The popular program solved a problem for urban children—how to engage and educate them about rural life and environmental issues, so that they understand both sides of a dilemma.

Using Your Intelligent Memory

Any time you spend improving your Intelligent Memory and using it in your daily life is a much better use of your memory than worrying about facts or faces you've forgotten. Your Intelligent Memory is one of the few abilities that gets better as time goes on, making it much more useful than ordinary memory, which not only worsens with age but can be easily replaced with a pencil and piece of paper. Nothing can substitute for our Intelligent Memory. It's one of our major strengths as human beings. Now that you appreciate it, get out there and exercise it wisely!

CHAPTER 12

Your Intelligent Memory Plan

Weaving exercises that strengthen your Intelligent Memory into your daily life isn't difficult. It's certainly not as difficult as physical exercise partly because most of the gear you need is already inside your head. However, the plan does require that you think more deliberately in advance about how you do things and make changes in your thinking.

To begin, think in small steps. As you've read, Intelligent Memory can work in almost any situation. It can tackle everything from the mundane, like solving a kitchen dilemma, to the monumental, like inspiring a major work of art. However, as a practical matter, most of us don't have the ego or free time, not to mention the skills, to plan a 30-year assault on a unified theory of relativity. You'll make more progress and prepare yourself better for eventually taking on major projects if you start with smaller, everyday problems that are more tractable and more likely to give you immediate satisfaction.

What problems are in front of you now? You want to get a digital camera but don't know what kind to get. One of your children is struggling with schoolwork and can barely keep up with classmates. You've got a nonrefundable plane ticket but can't make the trip. Your husband wants a dog but neither of you are home much. Your boss has asked you for ideas for next year's budget. Spam in your e-mail is making it impossible to read valid messages. Everyone's life is full of situations that a well-developed Intelligent Memory can make easier to resolve.

To remind yourself to keep exercising your Intelligent Memory and to gently motivate yourself, use a notebook. Notebooks have long been the secret weapon of not just successful writers and artists, but all sorts of thinkers and doers, like scientists and businesspeople. The notebooks of Leonardo da Vinci are famous as a record of his moment-to-moment thoughts and visual ideas. For Leonardo, these notebooks were a practical way of capturing ideas on the fly and reminding himself of his goals and progress toward those goals. Regardless of whether you intend to make a notebook public or use it only for private thoughts, you will find it to be an invaluable tool.

If you don't like using a notebook, another way to track your ideas and stimulate your thinking is to find someone to collaborate with or, short of that, someone willing to listen. A collaborator, whether a friend, family member, or someone you share a special interest with, like a fellow poet, is a wonderful source of ideas and directions and analysis. Talking to an audience is the method teachers use to teach themselves. For most of us, however, the notebook is the best way.

Keep in mind that your Intelligent Memory plan has several goals or purposes. You're trying to make sure that you give yourself enough motivation, time, and reward to flex your mental muscles. How much time and motivation is needed varies for different people. It's reasonable to plan on spending between 15 and 30 minutes a day. This is both the amount of time it takes to get up a head of speed in tackling Intelligent Memory–type problems and also about the most time people can devote to it in a day. This is also enough time so that you can see visible results day to day and benefit from the satisfaction of making real progress toward your goal. Practice using your Intelligent Memory in short bursts and not over prolonged periods. Think of it as a sprint, not a marathon. Most people can grab a few minutes of thinking time as they ride the subway, sit in a doctor's office, or wait for a pot of coffee to brew. If possible, pick the time of day you know your thoughts are the clearest and will flow most easily. If that's not possible, just realize that some times will be better than others. The most important first step is just devoting any time to strengthening Intelligent Memory.

Intelligent Memory has three major components to strengthen. Two of them are ideas and connections between ideas. This network of ideas and connections is the raw material you use to come up with better solutions to problems and more creative ideas and thoughts. The third component is critical thinking. Critical thinking shapes and selects the raw material from your thoughts, so you'll be able to recognize which solutions and thoughts work better. Which part of your Intelligent Memory needs the most strengthening at any one time depends on you.

Do you already have a wild imagination, but your great ideas never seem to go anywhere? Perhaps you need to work on critical thinking first. Do you have a problem coming up with ideas yourself, but find it easy to see what's wrong with those of others? Then maybe you should work on expanding connections. Perhaps you come up with ideas, but find fault with them right away. Or perhaps you're stuck in the middle of a problem right now. You may need more exuberant thinking, more creative solutions. Give yourself a brief period of mental freedom and permission to let your thoughts sprout and bloom. Later you can trim and harness them.

Here are some ways of jump-starting these different parts of your Intelligent Memory program:

1. **More Ideas:** If you need more possibilities to consider, scramble the elements or pieces of information you're using. Think backward through a process, eliminate an item, add something totally new, or simplify. Make a diagram of the problem, list the characteristics of each element, think of an analogous problem, or gather more information. Expose yourself to new sources of ideas. Surf through the cable channels to watch an unfamiliar television program or set your car radio on scan and listen to stations you haven't heard before. Go to a bookstore for different magazines or newspapers. Go to museums you've never visited before. Read randomly through useful reference books, like a book of quotations, a visual dictionary, or a world almanac. Do a Google search on the Web for items or people that happen to catch your fancy, or just for word combinations you think may be related to your problem. Do something new—take a route to work you've never traveled before,

talk to a stranger, eat an exotic food, read an author you've never read, write a limerick, or visit a store you've never been in.

2. **Break Out of Functional Fixedness:** If you feel fixated on a solution or way of doing something, try breaking the problem into smaller problems. Think about only the smaller part of the problem. Redefine your goal or change the order of the steps you take to do something. Instead of thinking about the problem and how to make something happen, try thinking about the exact opposite of the problem and how you'd stop that result from happening. Free-associate into a tape recorder or doodle on a notepad. Study a common object, like a pen, flower vase, or bar of soap, and try thinking of different uses for it. Examine the tools you're using and think about how you can employ them in ways they weren't intended.

3. **Look for Unusual Connections:** New connections can be found when you loosen your thinking about problems. One way to do this is by brainstorming. Forget for a moment analytical thinking. Forget for a time the problem itself (your Intelligent Memory won't, so you won't get totally off base). Try to stir creative ideas using any or all of the methods we've mentioned earlier. Try using visual aids. Look through an art or photography book, examine the advertisements in a magazine, think about the last movie you saw and imagine different endings. Look for solutions in the titles of country-and-western songs.

4. **Question Your Thinking:** Think about the assumptions you've applied to a problem. Ask whether they are valid or true. You may have made flawed assumptions about motives, abilities, or desires; what resources are available; timetables or schedules; or outcomes and goals. Examine your thinking for biases that may have crept in. Your thinking and conclusions may have been swayed by flawed logic, someone or something you saw or read, or a previous experience. Biases aren't necessarily bad, except when we are not aware that they are influencing our thinking. Think about the goal you are aiming for—is it still worthwhile or does it need redefining?

5. **Slow Your Thinking:** Consider the mental steps you took to reach a conclusion and ask whether any of these steps involved a hunch or guess or instinct. Hunches and other mental shortcuts tend to be shoot-from-the-hip thoughts, and not the slow, deliberate mental processes new problems require. Pause also to make sure you've included all the information you have or can get about a problem.

6. **Acquire Critical Thinking Tools:** These are the laws of logic and probability, and there are many of them you could or should have in your mental toolbox. However, for most people, a couple of the more general rules are quite useful in thinking through a variety of problems. Some valuable ones for most of the situations people face include: Remember that things do happen by chance. Even if the chance is small, if there's enough opportunities or enough time, even the most unlikely possibility can occur by chance alone. Be on guard to distinguish correlation from cause. Just because two events occur at more or less the same time, one did not necessarily cause the other. Another one of the rules of chance is the law of large numbers—evidence, whether from experience or studies, carries more weight when it is based on many cases, and not just a few, because just a few are more likely to be due to chance. Watch out for absolutes like "never" and "all." Remember that almost anything that can be good also has risks, so almost any action involves trade-offs. Think about those trade-offs. Beware of sunk-cost reasoning—how much you've already invested in a situation doesn't matter; it's how much you have at the moment that should be your basis for thinking about problems.

7. **Check Your Results:** Examine your solution or answer: Does it work immediately? Is it permanent? Is it practical? Is it affordable? Consider the consequences of your solution. A solution that looks good at first may produce disastrous ripple effects. A key question is whether your solution is truly an improvement or something you've opted for merely to get the problem out of your hair. One

way to check your results is to retrace and examine each step that got you there in order to ensure that the ultimate solution is on solid ground.

8. **Don't Be Too Hard on Yourself:** Even the best thinkers spin out hundreds if not thousands of ideas for every one that ever merits further notice. You aren't likely to do better, so accept this necessary inefficiency in the process. Remember that your Intelligent Memory will flow best if it's stressed a bit, but not too stressed. Too much stress and it will lock up (in sports terms, "choke"). Try to give yourself enough time, or pace yourself, so you don't have to face emergency situations while you're trying to improve your Intelligent Memory. Take breaks, not from thinking but from thinking about the problem directly. Recall that even if your mind goes in a totally different direction, that new direction may help your Intelligent Memory refresh connections that will do you good in the longer run. At the very least, don't expect your Intelligent Memory to work at its best under too much pressure.

9. **Fun Will Fight Mental Flab Too:** Building up your Intelligent Memory can be work, but it doesn't have to be. Anything you are really interested in, anything that fascinates you, any leads you pursue, will strengthen your Intelligent Memory.

10. **Just Start Thinking:** This is the most important tip of all. Anything that you do will help. Start with anything, anywhere. If you're standing at the bus stop, wonder: Why are manhole covers round and not square? Why can a bus be late or on time but never early? What are the advantages of a backpack over a briefcase? Why is that person dressed the way that she is? What are people reading? What is that loud music coming from a car radio? Start anywhere or anytime you find yourself with a free moment.

Start now!

NOTES AND SOURCES

What we call Intelligent Memory is a synthesis of evidence from a number of fields that have generally been distinct. For the reader wishing to delve into these areas more deeply, the following are useful starting points. For the neuroscience of basic neuronal processes in learning, see Fahle and Poggio's *Perceptual Learning* (Bradford, 2002). Implicit, unconscious memory and mental processes have been contrasted with explicit, conscious ones many times. Good recent compendia and reviews include: French and Cleeremans, *Implicit Learning and Consciousness* (Psychology Press, 2002); Kirsner, Speelman, Maybery, O'Brien-Malone, Anderson, and MacLeod (eds.), *Implicit and Explicit Mental Processes* (Lawrence Erlbaum, 1998); and Stadler and Frensch (eds.), *Handbook of Implicit Learning* (Sage Publications, 1998).

More popular treatments include Ornstein, *Multimind* (Houghton Mifflin, 1986); Claxton, *Hare Brain, Tortoise Mind* (Fourth Estate, 1997); and Bransford and Stein, *Ideal Problem Solver* (W. H. Freeman and Co., 1984). These latter books also get into everyday thinking and creativity. More scholarly recent approaches to the mental processes involved in everyday-life activities can be found in Reason, *Human Error* (Cambridge University Press, 1990), and Wohl, *Everyday Thinking: Memory, Reasoning and Judgment in the Real World* (Lawrence Erlbaum, 2002).

Better strategies for critical thinking are covered by Halpern, *Thought and Knowledge,* 3rd ed. (Lawrence Erlbaum, 1996). Theoretical perspectives on some of the same issues are in Baron, *Thinking and Deciding,* 2nd ed. (Cambridge University Press, 1994), and Oaksford and Chater (eds.), *Rational Models of Cognition* (Oxford University Press, 1998). Creativity is reviewed scientifically in Sternberg (ed.), *Handbook of Creativity* (Cambridge University Press, 1999), and Ward, Smith, and Vaid (eds.), *Creative Thought* (American Psychological Association Press, 1997). Scientifically proven strategies to improve creativity are given in

Ward, Finke, and Smith, *Creativity and the Mind: Discovering the Genius Within* (Plenum, 1995). Mankoff's *The Naked Cartoonist* (Black Dog and Leventhal, 2002) has a narrower perspective but is perhaps more fun to read. Dean Simonton has been exploring the metric of creativity and genius through historical studies for some time; his *Genius and Creativity: Selected Papers* (Ablex, 1997) brings together some of his professional publications, while his *Origins of Genius: Darwinian Perspectives on Creativity* (Oxford University Press, 1999) is a more unified account.

This list is hardly exhaustive of the sources used and that you might use; the chapter reference notes give more specifics. We don't necessarily agree with every opinion in these sources, of course. Also, the reader should realize that technical works often focus primarily on controversial topics or points. What is generally accepted may barely appear in scientific publications and thus may be almost invisible to the lay reader.

Introduction

xii   **In a study of how people**   Ceci, S., and J. Liker. 1986. "A Day at the Races: A Study of IQ, Expertise, and Cognitive Complexity." *Journal of Experimental Psychology* 115:255–266.

xiii   **One company head asks**   "Working," *Smart Money,* March 2001, p. 140.

Chapter 1: What Is Intelligent Memory?

2   **A perfect example**   Doyle, Arthur Conan. 1887. *A Study in Scarlet.* New York: J. H. Sears and Co.

Chapter 2: Testing Your Intelligent Memory

14   **Watson and Sherlock Holmes go camping**   Wardell, D. J. "Funniest Joke." www.wardell.org.

23   **Do you understand**   Andrews, S. and D. Scarratt. 1998. "Rule and Analogy Mechanisms in Reading Nonwords—Hough Dou Peapel Rede New Wirds?" *Journal of Experimental Psychology: Human Perception and Performance* 24: 1052–1086.

30   **neurotica**   Margolis, S. 2000. *Neurotica.* New York: Bantam Books.

30   **lipshtick**   Macsai, G. 2001. *Lipshtick.* New York: HarperCollins.

30   **Are vegetarians allowed**   Carlin, G. 1997. *Brain Droppings.* New York: Hyperion.

37   **Students were given the following instructions**   Finke, R., T. Ward, and

S. Smith. 1992. *Creative Cognition—Theory, Research and Applications.* Cambridge, MA: MIT Press, p. 153.

Chapter 3: Improving Your Intelligent Memory

45 **However, it imposes a major limitation** The actual number is debated, and there are reasons to believe it is less, perhaps around 3 to 4. Nelson Cowan, in "The Magical Number 4 in Short-Term Memory: A Reconsideration of Mental Storage Capacity" (2000, *Behavioral and Brain Sciences* 24:87–185), gives a cogent review of the evidence. However, for our purposes, the exact limitation is not as important as the fact that there is a limit on the maximum amount, and that it is surprisingly small. This limited-capacity system is a major bottleneck for all of our thinking.

Chapter 4: Enhancing Attention

50 **In a study of attention** Gordon, B. 1995. *Memory, Remembering and Forgetting in Everyday Life.* New York: Mastermedia, p. 275.

52 **The experts remembered the positions** Chase, W., and H. Simon. 1973. "Perception in Chess." *Cognitive Psychology* 4:55–81.

52 **Students in a Chicago high school** Csikszentmihalyi, M. 1992. "Reviews and Response." In *Technologies for the 21st Century,* M. Greenberger, ed. Santa Monica: The Voyager Company, p. 32.

53 **This happens at the university** 2003. *New York Times.* January 2.

54 **In 2001, scientists at Carnegie Mellon** 2001. *New York Times.* July 31.

56 **When astronaut Jerry Linenger** Bush, C. 2001. "How to Multitask." *New York Times Magazine.* April 8.

58 **The training that U.S. Marine snipers** 2001. "Licensed to Kill: Marine Sniper Waits for the Perfect Moment." *Wall Street Journal.* December 21.

59 **Readers delighted** Asimov, I. 1979. *Isaac Asimov's Book of Facts.* New York: Wing Books, p. 54.

59 **Many foods cost too much** Bransford, J., and B. Stein. 1993. *The Ideal Problem Solver: A Guide for Improving Thinking, Learning, and Creativity* (2nd ed.). New York: W. H. Freeman and Co., p. 138.

60 **The "cocktail party effect"** Wood, N., and N. Cowan. 1995. "The Cocktail Party Phenomenon Revisited: Attention and Memory in the Procedure of Cherry 1953." *Journal of Experimental Psychology: Learning, Memory and Cognition* 21 (1): 255.

61 **Whom do you see in this picture?** Cecil Stoughton, White House/John F. Kennedy Library, Boston, MA.

62   **You are the driver of a bus**   Bransford and Stein. *The Ideal Problem Solver,* p. 156.

66   **Look at this block of randomly**   Lapp, D. 1987. *Don't Forget.* Reading, Massachuetts: Perseus books, p. 4.

66   **Seconds later, a silky voice answered**   Allen, W. 1975. "The Whore of Mensa." *Without Feathers.* New York: Ballantine Books, p. 35.

Chapter 5: Expanding Scratch-Pad Memory

69   **There was a strong noise**   Baddeley, A. 1999. *Essentials of Human Memory.* East Sussex, UK: Psychology Press, p. 67.

70   **Word recall test**   Baddeley, A. 1996. *Your Memory: A User's Guide.* London: Prion, p. 81.

72   **He strode across the court**   Baddeley, A. *Your Memory: A User's Guide,* p. 169.

73   **The psychologist who first**   Miller, G. 1955. "The Magical Number Seven, Plus or Minus Two—Some Limits on Our Capacity for Processing Information." *Psychological Review* 101:2, 343–352.

74   **This is how a Russian psychologist**   Luria, A. 1968. *The Mind of a Mnemonist.* New York: Avon Books, p. 66.

75   **S.F., a college student**   Chase, W., and K. A. Ericsson. 1981. "Skilled Memory." In *Cognitive Skills and Their Acquisition,* J. R. Anderson, ed. Mahwah, NJ: Lawrence Erlbaum Associates, p. 141.

78   **Researchers learned this by studying**   Ericsson, K., and P. Polson. 1988. "An Experimental Analysis of the Mechanics of a Memory Skill." *Journal of Experimental Psychology* 14:305–316.

81   **Sitting with Bob**   adapted from Daneman, M., and P. Carpenter. 1980. "Individual Differences in Working Memory and Reading." *Journal of Verbal Learning and Verbal Behavior* 19:450–466.

83   **This exercise shows an assortment**   Gamon, D., and A. Bragdon. 1998. *Building Mental Muscle.* San Francisco: Brainwaves Books, p. 136.

85   **Here's a grid**   Gamon, D. and A. Bragdon. *Building Mental Muscle,* p. 127.

85   **This exercise is intended**   Baddeley, A., et al. 1975. "Word Length and the Structure of Short-Term Memory." *Journal of Verbal Learning and Verbal Behavior* 14:575–589.

Chapter 6: Storing More Memories

88   **In one test of the capacity**   Haber, R. 1970. "How We Remember What We See." *Scientific American,* May, p. 105.

88   Fifty years after taking high school Spanish   Bahrick, H. 2000. "Long-Term Maintenance of Knowledge." In *The Oxford Handbook of Memory*, E. Tulving and F. Craik, eds. New York: Oxford University Press, p. 347.

90   The procedure is actually quite simple   Bransford, J. 1979. *Human Cognition—Learning, Understanding and Remembering*. Belmont, CA: Wadsworth Publishing Co., p. 134.

92   One study asked actors   Noice, H., and T. Noice. 1996. "Two Approaches to Learning a Theatrical Script." *Memory* 4 (1): 1–17.

93   Even people with extraordinary memories   Luria, A. 1968. *The Mind of a Mnemonist*. New York: Avon Books, p. 49.

95   To see how well elaborating   Bransford. J., and B. Stein. 1993. *The Ideal Problem Solver: A Guide for Improving Thinking, Learning, and Creativity* (2nd ed.). New York: W. H. Freeman and Co., p. 138.

98   This was the method used   Maguire, E., et al. 2003. "Routes to Remembering: The Brains Behind Superior Memory." *Nature Neuroscience*. Vol. 6, no. 1, January p. 90.

99   A pair of numbers is   Wilding, J., and E. Valentine. 1996. "Memory Expertise." *Basic and Applied Memory Research: Theory in Context*. Vol. I. Mahwah, NJ: Lawrence Erlbaum Associates, p. 399.

99   Mel Brooks and Anne Bancroft   Noice and Noice. "Two Approaches to Learning a Theatrical Script."

99   Scans of an expert and novice   Groeger, J. 2000. *Understanding Driving*. East Sussex, UK: Psychology Press.

101   A few years ago, British letter carriers   Baddeley, A. 1996. *Your Memory: A User's Guide*. London: Prion, p. 27.

102   Storing memories from   Stickgold, R., et al. 2001. "Sleep, Learning, and Dreams: Off-line Memory Reprocessing." *Science*, Vol. 294, November 2; Heuer, H., et al. 1998 "Effects of Sleep Loss, Time of Day, and Extended Mental Work on Implicit and Explicit Learning of Sequences." *Journal of Experimental Psychology: Applied*, 4(2): 139–162.

103   Following are two sets   Baddeley, A. *Your Memory*, p. 76.

104   Finding a category   Bransford and Stein. *The Ideal Problem Solver*, p. 134.

Chapter 7: Sparking Connections

108   Two gentlemen   Asimov, I. 1971. *Treasury of Humor*. Boston, MA: Houghton Mifflin Company, p. 167.

108   Jones was having   Asimov, I. *Treasury of Humor*, p. 69.

110   Yet another way of understanding the kinds of connections   Adapted from Whitaker, H. 1976. "A Case of the Isolation of the Language Func-

tion," in *Studies in Neurolinguistics*. Vol. 2. H. Whitaker, ed. New York: Academic Press.

112   **Such thinking has given us**   Manning, A. 2001. "New Meaning to 'Patently Absurd,'" *USA Today*, July 30.

113   **Thomas Edison obtained patents**   Simonton, D. 1997. "Creative Productivity: A Predictive and Explanatory Model of Career Trajectories and Landmarks." *Psychological Review* 104 (1): 66–89.

114   **You'll be asked to apply**   Perkins, D. 2000. *Archimedes' Bathtub: The Art and Logic of Breakthrough Thinking*. New York: W. W. Norton and Co., p. 39.

114   **A new design for the roof**   Mayer, R. 1992. *Thinking, Problem Solving, Cognition*. New York: W. H. Freeman and Co., p. 367.

115   **When Ben Franklin was designing**   Holyoak, K., and P. Thagard. 1995. *Mental Leaps: Analogy in Creative Thought*. Cambridge, MA: MIT Press, p. 185.

115   **When the architect Frank Gehry**   White, S. 2002. *New Ideas About New Ideas*. New York: Perseus Publishing.

115   **The managers of a dating service**   Kurlantzick, J. 2001. "Hello, Goodbye, Hey Maybe I Love You?" *U.S. News & World Report*, June 4.

115   **As a result, the company designed**   Halpern, D. 1996. *Thought and Knowledge: An Introduction to Critical Thinking*. Mahwah, NJ: Lawrence Erlbaum Associates, p. 350.

116   **The tricuspid valve**   Kelley, T., and J. Littman. 2001. *The Art of Innovation*. New York: Doubleday, p. 48.

116   **Envisioning a thief trying**   Freeman, A., and B. Golden. 1997. *Why Didn't I Think of That?: Bizarre Origins of Ingenious Inventions We Couldn't Live Without*. New York: John Wiley and Sons, p. 70.

116   **One of the most famous wild imaginings**   Bransford. J., and B. Stein. 1993. *The Ideal Problem Solver: A Guide for Improving, Thinking, Learning, and Creativity* (2nd ed.). New York: W. H. Freeman and Co., p. 68.

117   **Having seen this analogy**   Dunker, K. 1945. "On Problem Solving." In *Thinking and Reasoning*. 1968. New York: Penguin Books, p. 28.

119   **The principles are the same**   Osborn, A. 1953. *Applied Imagination*. New York: Charles Scribner's Sons, p. 248.

120   **Don't drive with your brakes on**   Parnes, S., and H. Harding. 1962. *A Source Book for Creative Thinking*. New York: Charles Scribner's Sons, p. 288.

120   **The designers at the product design**   Kelley and Littman. *The Art of Innovation*, p. 10.

121   **Of course, you don't have to be asleep**   Osborn, A. *Applied Imagination*, p. 160.

121   **William Hewlett, one of the founders**   2001. *Forbes*, December 10.

Chapter 8: Solving Problems

130   **And even though people think**   Brickman, P., et al. 1978. "Lottery Winners and Accident Victims: Is Happiness Relative?" *Journal of Personality and Social Psychology* 36: 917–927.

133   **Following are two lists**   Gleitman, H., A. Fridlung, D. Reisberg. 2000. *Basic Psychology.* New York: Norton, p. 230.

135   **Executives at an advertising agency**   Jaffe, G. 2001. "With Recruiting Slow, the Air Force Seeks a New Ad Campaign." *Wall Street Journal,* February 14.

136   **The French made this mistake**   "A Brief History of the Maginot Line." www.geocities.com.

136   **After September 11**   2001. *Variety,* October 8.

137   **Reading aloud is a good way**   Hauser, S. 2001. "Reading? It's for the Dogs." *Wall Street Journal,* August 9.

138   **Charles Darwin struggled for years**   Desmond, A., and J. Moore. 1991. *Darwin: The Life of a Tormented Evolutionist.* New York: W. W. Norton and Co., p. 467; "Dr. Alfred Russel Wallace at Home," an interview by E. Rann, *Pall Mall,* March 1909.

138   **One of the greatest innovations**   "Fosbury, Dick." www.britannica.com.

140   **Here are two problems**   Maier, N. 1931. "Reasoning in Humans." In *Thinking and Reasoning.* 1968. P. Wason and P. Johnson-Laird, eds. New York: Penguin Books, p. 17.

140   **On a table is a candle**   Dunker, K. 1945. "On Problem Solving." In *Thinking and Reasoning.* 1968. New York: Penguin Books, p. 28.

142   **You are presented with two jars**   Denes-Raj, V., and S. Epstein. 1994. "Conflict Between Intuitive and Rational Processing: When People Behave Against Their Better Judgment." *Journal of Personality and Social Psychology* 66 (5): 819–829.

143   **Here's an example of how**   Claxton, G. 1997. *Hare Brain, Tortoise Mind: How Intelligence Increases When You Think Less.* New York: Ecco Press, p. 52. One form of the formula is given in Claxton's book.

144   **Jack Kilby was a young electrical engineer**   Reid, T. 2000. "Mister Chips." *Washington Post Magazine,* December 20.

145   **Taking a lemon and making lemonade**   Barta, P. 2002. "Jailhouse Conversion: Ossining Tires of Being a Prisoner to Sing Sing." *Wall Street Journal,* March 29.

145   **The English doctor Edward Jenner**   Porter, R., Ed., *Medicine of Healing.* 1997. New York: Marlowe and Company.

145   **Finding a solution happens**   Bransford. J., and B. Stein. 1993. *The Ideal Problem Solver: A Guide for Improving Thinking, Learning, and Creativity* (2nd ed.). New York: W. H. Freeman and Co.

147   **The director of creative strategy at Hallmark**   Wilson, C. 2001. "Hallmark Hits the Mark," *USA Today,* June 14.

147   **Take this wild**   Cohen, G. 1989. *Memory in the Real World.* Mahwah, NJ: Lawrence Erlbaum Associates, p. 154.

148   **See if you can catch**   Seifert, C., et al. 1995. "Demystification of Cognitive Insight: Opportunistic Assimilation and the Prepared-Mind Perspective." In *The Nature of Insight.* R. Sternberg and J. Davidson, eds. Cambridge, MA: MIT Press, p. 65.

149   **This was the position a swimsuit manufacturer**   Harris, R. "Virtual Salt." www.virtualsalt.com/crebook4.htm.

149   **These problems require**   Metcalfe, J., and D. Wiebe. 1987. "Intuition in Insight and Noninsight Problem Solving." *Memory and Cognition* 15(3): 238–246.

153   **This exercise tests**   Adapted from Bowers, G.H., et al. 1990. "Intuition in the Context of Discovery." *Cognitive Psychology* 22: 79–109.

154   **When the city of London**   Harris, R. "Virtual Salt." www.virtualsalt.com/crebook2.htm; Bransford and Stein. *Ideal Problem Solver,* p. 164.

154   **Sally let loose**   Bransford and Stein. *Ideal Problem Solver,* p. 164.

155   **A wealthy merchant**   Lewis, D., and J. Greene. 1982. *Thinking Better.* New York: Rawson, Wade Publishers, p. 198.

Chapter 9: Working Creatively

157   **This misconception comes**   Mayer, R. E. 1999. "Fifty Years of Creativity Research." In *Handbook of Creativity,* R. S. Sternberg, ed. Cambridge: Cambridge University Press, pp. 449ff.

158   **Alan Lightman**   Lightman, A. 2002. "The Art of Science." *New Scientist,* vol. 176, p. 68.

159   **The Cartoonist**   Ziegler, J. In Robert Mankoff. 2002. *The Naked Cartoonist.* New York: Black Dog & Leventhal, pp. 134–135.

160   **The Writer**   Donaldson, S. R. 1991. *The Gap into Conflict: The Real Story.* New York: Bantam, pp. 222–223.

161   **Photographer Cindy Sherman**   1997. *Cindy Sherman: Retrospective.* New York: Thames & Hudson, p. 184.

161   **Jackson Pollock**   1956. "Pollock Style:" *Time,* August 20.

161   **He was also filmed**   Ratcliff, C. 1998. *The Fate of a Gesture.* Boulder, CO: Westview Press, p. 111. Pollock's painting methods are analyzed in detail by Pepe Karmel in "Pollock at Work: The Films and Photographs of Hans Namuth" (1998. *Jackson Pollock.* K. Varnedoe, P. Karmel, eds. New York: Museum of Modern Art).

162   **Dashiell Hammett**   Hellman, L. 1965. "Dashiell Hammett: A Memoir." *New York Review of Books,* November 25.

Chapter 10: Preventing Mental Mistakes

166   **In one case, a man was accused**   Schacter, D. 2001. *The Seven Sins of Memory.* Boston, MA: Houghton Mifflin Company, p. 92.

166   **A night clerk devised**   "Clerk's Scheme to Steal Cash Overlooks Significant Detail," 2000. *Kansas City Star.* September 7.

166   **Three maintenance men**   Northcutt, W. 2000. *The Darwin Awards.* New York: Dutton, p. 42.

169   **This is a two-player game**   Bransford. J., and B. Stein. 1993. *The Ideal Problem Solver: A Guide for Improving, Thinking, Learning, and Creativity* (2nd ed.). New York: W. H. Freeman and Co., p. 182.

170   **Psychologists surveying teenagers**   Kruger, J., and D. Dunning.1999. "Unskilled and Unaware of It—How Difficulties in Recognizing One's Own Incompetence Lead to Inflated Self-Assessments. *Journal of Personality and Social Psychology* 77(6): 1121–1134.

170   **In one survey**   Gibbs, N. and M. Duffy. 2000. "Bush and Gore: Two Men, Two Visions." *Time* online edition, October 28.

171   **Jana Novotna was playing**   Gladwell, M. 2000. "The Art of Failure." *New Yorker,* August 21 p. 84.

173   **There are 40**   Halper, D. 1996. *Thought and Knowledge: An Introduction to Critical Thinking.* Mahwah, NJ: Lawrence Erlbaum Associates, p. 260; and Levy, D. 1997. *Tools of Critical Thinking.* Needham Heights, MA: Allyn and Bacon, p. 180.

174   **People have a fear**   "In Brief." 2002. *New Scientist,* June, vol. 174, p. 25.

174   **A woman walks into a psychiatrist's office**   Levy, D. *Tools of Critical Thinking.* p. 157.

175   **Martin Gardner**   Gardner, M. 1996. *The Night Is Large.* New York: St. Martin's Press, p. 481.

175   **A man in Cedar Rapids**   "Least Competent Criminals," 2001. *News of the Weird,* October 10.

176   **Working alone, Tom can mow**   Halpern, D., *Thought and Knowledge,* p. 29.

176   **A man in Toronto**   Northcutt, W. *The Darwin Awards,* p. 150.

177   **Imagine it's two in the morning**   Bransford and Stein. *The Ideal Problem Solver,* p. 23.

177   **The problem of the divorced father**   Blanchard-Fields, F., et al. 1995. "Age Differences in Problem-Solving Style: The Role of Emotional Salience." *Psychology and Aging* 10 (2): 173–180.

178   **You're driving alone at night**   Halpern, D. *Thought and Knowledge*, p. 318.

179   **The following solutions were proposed**   Marchetti, M. 2000. "Wild Pitches." *Smart Money*, December 19.

179   **Connect the dots**   Wason, P., and P. Johnson-Laird, eds. 1968. "Reasoning in Humans." *Thinking and Reasoning*, New York: Penguin Books.

180   **For each pair**   Halpern, D., *Thought and Knowledge*, p. 270.

181   **A town is served**   Claxton, G. 1997. *Hare Brain, Tortoise Mind: How Intelligence Increases When You Think Less*. New York: Ecco Press, p. 55.

181   **You're on a weight-loss program**   Mayer, R. 1992. *Thinking, Problem Solving, Cognition*, New York: W. H. Freeman and Co., p. 491.

182   **What's wrong with this picture?**   Pricken, M. 2002. *Creative Advertising*. London: Thames and Hudson, p. 62. From advertisement captioned "The vitamin supplement for animals with nutritional deficiencies." Client: FCL Laboratories (Enervit). Agency: TBWA, Barcelona. Creative Direction: Xavi Munill. Art Direction: Tomas Descals.

Chapter 11: Ideas for Using Intelligent Memory

185   **An Inspired Fix**   Weisberg, R. 1986. *Creativity*. New York: W. H. Freeman and Co., p. 4.

187   **Cancer Scare**   Baron, J. 1988. *Thinking and Deciding*. Cambridge, UK: Cambridge University Press, p. 186.

189   **Managing a Grocery Store**   Bransford. J., and B. Stein. 1993. *The Ideal Problem Solver: A Guide for Improving, Thinking, Learning, and Creativity* (2nd ed.). New York: W. H. Freeman and Co., p. 55.

191   **Getting a Better Job**   Sternberg, R. 1997. *Successful Intelligence*. New York: Plume, p. 208.

191   **Smart Trash**   Sternberg, R., et al. 2000. *Practical Intelligence in Everyday Life*. Cambridge, UK: Cambridge University Press, p. 32.

192   **An Inspiration from Childhood**   2001. "James F. Bradley, 81." *Baltimore Sun*, April 11.

193   **The Boss Who Stayed Late**   Sternberg, R. et al. 2000. *Practical Intelligence*, p. 209.

194   **Soaking Up a New Idea**   Freeman, A., and B. Golden, 1997. *Why Didn't I Think of That?: Bizarre Origins of Ingenious Inventions We Couldn't Live Without*. New York: John Wiley and Sons, p. 41.

195   **From Toys to Art**   Weisberg, R. *Creativity*, p. 111.

196   **Finding Gold**   Kinder, G. 1998. *Ship of Gold in the Deep Blue Sea*. New York: Atlantic Monthly Press, p. 476.

197   **A Quicker Way to Gas Up**   Weber, T. 2001. "The New Way to Shop." *Wall Street Journal,* February 27.

198   **Helping a Movie Star Cope with Pain**   MacFarquhar, L. 2001. "The Producer." *New Yorker,* October 15.

200   **The Noisy Apartment**   Ruggiero, V. 1998. *The Art of Thinking.* New York: Addison-Wesley Educational Publishers, p. 114.

201   **Equal Time**   Strassel, K. 2002. "Hug a Logger, Not a Tree." *Wall Street Journal,* May 23.

FOR THE BEST IN PAPERBACKS, LOOK FOR THE

In every corner of the world, on every subject under the sun, Penguin represents quality and variety—the very best in publishing today.

For complete information about books available from Penguin—including Penguin Classics, Penguin Compass, and Puffins—and how to order them, write to us at the appropriate address below. Please note that for copyright reasons the selection of books varies from country to country.

In the United States: Please write to *Penguin Group (USA), P.O. Box 12289 Dept. B, Newark, New Jersey 07101-5289* or call 1-800-788-6262.

In the United Kingdom: Please write to *Dept. EP, Penguin Books Ltd, Bath Road, Harmondsworth, West Drayton, Middlesex UB7 0DA.*

In Canada: Please write to *Penguin Books Canada Ltd, 10 Alcorn Avenue, Suite 300, Toronto, Ontario M4V 3B2.*

In Australia: Please write to *Penguin Books Australia Ltd, P.O. Box 257, Ringwood, Victoria 3134.*

In New Zealand: Please write to *Penguin Books (NZ) Ltd, Private Bag 102902, North Shore Mail Centre, Auckland 10.*

In India: Please write to *Penguin Books India Pvt Ltd, 11 Panchsheel Shopping Centre, Panchsheel Park, New Delhi 110 017.*

In the Netherlands: Please write to *Penguin Books Netherlands bv, Postbus 3507, NL-1001 AH Amsterdam.*

In Germany: Please write to *Penguin Books Deutschland GmbH, Metzlerstrasse 26, 60594 Frankfurt am Main.*

In Spain: Please write to *Penguin Books S. A., Bravo Murillo 19, 1° B, 28015 Madrid.*

In Italy: Please write to *Penguin Italia s.r.l., Via Benedetto Croce 2, 20094 Corsico, Milano.*

In France: Please write to *Penguin France, Le Carré Wilson, 62 rue Benjamin Baillaud, 31500 Toulouse.*

In Japan: Please write to *Penguin Books Japan Ltd, Kaneko Building, 2-3-25 Koraku, Bunkyo-Ku, Tokyo 112.*

In South Africa: Please write to *Penguin Books South Africa (Pty) Ltd, Private Bag X14, Parkview, 2122 Johannesburg.*